flying finn

Stephen Davison

BLACKSTAFF
PRESS

BELFAST

'Well, what's the craic?'

Those were the first words that Martin Finnegan said to me when we met for the first time at the Cookstown 100 in 2003. I had been watching him working underneath his race truck in the paddock and as he crawled out he hailed me with that familiar Irish greeting. It was to be the beginning of a lot of craic.

Although I had already noticed and photographed Martin's exploits on the track, when I met him at Cookstown it was the first time that I had seen him without his helmet on. Martin's easy charm relaxed everyone into his company and within a few minutes we were chatting away about racing and photography as if we had known each other for years.

Almost from the word go Martin was asking me how he could get more media coverage for his racing. He was at the 'up and coming' stage of his career and, as was so typical of him, he was in a hurry to make progress. Unlike many people in road racing, Martin understood the value of publicity in attracting and repaying loyal sponsors. He cared about his team's presentation and image and wanted to use them to gain coverage. Knowing that I worked for the racing magazines, Martin sought my advice as to how he could get their attention and he understood completely when I said that the one sure way that would guarantee the media could not ignore him was to win. He had no intention of doing anything else.

From the 2003 season onwards Martin began to mix it with the established stars of the game in all of the major events. Every weekend he was filling my lens from the front of the pack. It quickly became obvious that Martin was not just very fast on a motorcycle but that he also had a unique control that allowed him to ride in an incredibly exciting style. That style became even more spectacular as he became familiar with the bends and bumps of the Irish and Manx road racing courses over the next few seasons. Even when he did not win Martin Finnegan often made the best photograph.

We soon became good friends as I was drawn in by Martin's easy-going nature and his brilliance on a bike. He wanted to win races and catch headlines and I wanted to capture the very best bike racing images that I could. We travelled the world living the road racing life to the full, racing and photographing it in the same way.

It never ceased to amaze me how Martin, no matter how fast he was going, could spot me around the course whether I was buried in an Irish hedge or hiding behind the Macau armco. Before a race, he would take the time to point out to me the best spots to capture a big jump or a crossed-up wheelie. With that kind of knowledge allied to his stunning skill it is hardly surprising that Martin provided the best action shots of my career.

It wasn't just on the track that Martin was amenable to the camera. He understood that I was interested in his life away from bikes and how that influenced his racing. To get good photographs a photographer needs good access and down the years I was able to watch quietly with my camera as he prepared his machines for racing or trained his body for the stresses and strains of the battle on the track. Nor was the personal side of his life shut away – he invited me to his home to meet his infinitely hospitable family, to his work on the plant machinery that he serviced, to his wedding with Brenda and as he played with their daughter Rachel. It was a great privilege to be part of so many of those bright days.

When you are allowed into someone's life to see how much a man like Martin means to the people around him, you also understand something of the pain and anguish that engulfs them when he is no longer there. Martin's family were fully aware of the dangers that motorcycle road racing holds but nothing could have prepared them for the loss they were to suffer at Tandragee on 3 May 2008 when Martin died in a crash at Marlacoo corner on the second lap of the 600cc race. Nor can I fully believe that it has happened myself.

Martin was very happy that May morning as I photographed him on the grid before the race, as happy as I had ever seen him. I was at Cooley Hill during that tragic race, waiting for him to come into sight again, but he never came back. When I got to Marlacoo Martin's smashed bike was still lying on the bank where it had come to rest.

A few days later I stood outside the church in Lusk as his brothers carried his coffin through the gates. With the funeral ceremony over, the Finnegan family lined up by the graveside to receive the mourners' condolences. Martin's wife Brenda was at the head of the sad line and she whispered to me that she was happy that so much of Martin's life had been recorded. I made my way along to Martin's parents Margaret and Jim, his sisters Liz and Geraldine and his brothers Sean, Peter and James until finally I came to Paul.

'Maybe you have all the pictures you would need for a book about Martin, Stephen,' he said, as we shook hands.

Brenda's and Paul's words stayed with me as I walked out of that little country churchyard. There had always been an unspoken pact between Martin and I that some day we would do a book together on his career, but everything still had a long way to go. Not every race he wanted to win had been won, not every photograph I wanted to take had been taken. This book should never have been done without him; it should have been a shared enterprise as everything else had been.

As so often in this cruel sport of ours, it was not to be.

What we have now of Martin is all we have and it will not be allowed to fade away. Martin Finnegan was, simply, the most spectacular road racer the world has ever seen. More importantly, he was a man who lived the richest, fullest life imaginable. That he is now missed so much bears witness to that. It was a very great honour to have known him.

And to have shared all of that craic.

STEPHEN DAVISON

9

'He could become a bishop…'

When Martin Anthony Finnegan entered this world on the cold, autumn day of October the 8th, 1979, he arrived with two striking features that would catch the eye of everyone who would ever meet him thereafter.

'Martin was born with a full head of the thickest black hair and the biggest brown eyes you've ever seen,' his mother Margaret fondly remembers. 'The nurse said she thought that he looked like he could become a bishop one day!'

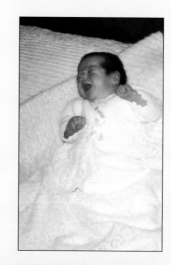

The last of Margaret and her husband Jim's seven children, Martin was sixteen years younger than his eldest sister Liz. In between were Geraldine, James, Paul, Sean and Peter, who provided their newborn brother with the warmth and security of a big Irish family when he was brought home to the village of Lusk, a few miles north of Dublin.

With so many older siblings Martin always had someone to look after him. 'We could hardly leave the house without taking him with us!' Liz and Geraldine remember. 'We always had him in the pram or by the hand when we were going anywhere.'

Used to getting plenty of attention and being at the centre of things as the baby of the family, Martin enjoyed the indulgence of everyone around him. 'He was ruined altogether,' Paul teases. 'On his first day at school he got a Mars bar and a bottle of Coke when the rest of us had had to have jam sandwiches!'

It would have been easy for Martin to become spoiled by all this attention but the down-to-earthness of the Finnegan family kept him firmly grounded. His father Jim, who worked long hours as a psychiatric nurse, instilled in all of his children the importance of hard work and the value of money. 'Money wasn't plentiful when the children were growing up, there was never much spare for any extravagances but there was always enough.'

When the time came, the youngest Finnegan followed the rest of the family to the nearby National school in Lusk village where he excelled. 'He was a bright youngster,' Geraldine recalls. 'And he was meticulous about his book work.'

Liz remembers the same attention to detail in Martin's schoolwork. 'When he was at St Finian's in Swords, I remember him coming home to me with a school project that he wanted typed up,' Liz says. 'He drove me mad with it because he stood over me watching every letter and if I made a mistake he wanted me to start the whole thing again! He was so fussy and neat about anything like that.'

School also provided Martin with his first taste of sporting competition. One of his teachers at Lusk was involved in the coaching of the Irish Olympic athletes and Martin was encouraged to train and to compete against his schoolmates.

Outside the family home in Lusk.

As a youngster Martin was quite lightly built, skinny even, and it wasn't until his late teens that he developed the strong physique that was to become so much a feature of his racing ability. In his teenage years Martin took up boxing and then judo. 'He enjoyed the competitiveness of the sports but he wasn't really aggressive enough for the actual fighting,' his brother Sean remembers. 'What Martin enjoyed most was the discipline and the training of both sports.'

After school Martin was rarely to be found sitting about the house. Like all of his brothers and sisters, he had little jobs in and around the village that earned him some pocket money. One of those jobs was just around the corner at Round Tower Plant, a company owned by Tony Carton who was also a well-known motorcycle road racer and sponsor. 'From about ten or eleven years old Martin was always about the yard and the workshop after school,' Tony recalls. 'He had a great way with him, always easy-going and chatting. A brainy kid too, ahead of his years. If the TV wasn't going right or if the water wasn't coming out of the tap, Martin would be working at it and could fix it.'

Eight-year-old Martin (front, centre) with his family – Elizabeth, James, Peter, his father Jim and mother Margaret, Sean, Geraldine and Paul.

The afternoons and evenings spent in Tony's workshop also introduced Martin to machinery and engineering, an interest that would grow into an apprenticeship with CIE, the Irish national railway company, when he finished school at seventeen.

Tony and Martin also shared a passionate interest in motorbikes, although initially Martin's involvement was in motocross rather than road racing.

From he was little more than a toddler Martin was taken to race meetings all over Ireland by his older sister

Martin Finnegan and Classic bike racer Maurice Wilson may have seemed unlikely friends but their lives were woven together through motorcycle racing. Martin first met Maurice, a friend of Tony Carton's and a fellow racer, at Round Tower Plant. They travelled to the races with Tony and the rest of the crew, including to Tandragee for Maurice's debut where this picture was taken. Martin was thirteen years old at the time. Three years later Maurice and Lorcan McGuinness were with Martin when he made his debut on tarmac at Mondello Park. They continued to meet at the races and give each other a helping hand until Maurice was sadly killed during practice at Tandragee in 2004. On the evening he died he was wearing a pair of Martin's racing leathers. Martin was killed in a crash on the same course four years later.

Geraldine. Geraldine's husband Alan raced in motocross and grass track events, and Martin and his older brothers Sean and Peter would eventually take up the sport.

A family friend, Fran McGuinness, bought Martin his first motocross bike when he was just eight years old and Martin immediately demonstrated his talent.

'Fran bought Martin an 80cc Yamaha and he brought it down to a field behind the house for Martin to try,' Sean says. 'I remember Fran falling down on to his knees laughing as he watched Martin going round and round. He just couldn't believe how well Martin could ride the wee bike and how fast he was on it. He was delighted.'

Now, with a bike of his own, Martin wanted to be out racing every weekend and his competitive motorcycle racing career began in 1990 when he rode the little Yamaha in a schoolboy race at Courtown in County Wexford. From that day on there was no holding him back as he progressed through the schoolboy ranks of the sport. 'We used to say every March, when the season started, that there would be no Sunday dinner until October,' Geraldine laughs.

Martin had one other hurdle to overcome before he could get to the racing though. Most of the motocross events took place on a Sunday but his mother was keen that Martin should continue to attend Mass in the local chapel, St MacCullin's. Martin, on the other hand, had bikes to sort and he would dodge chapel. 'One Sunday he came back home and Mam asked him how had Mass gone,' his brother Peter laughs as he remembers.

'Martin said it had been fine and Mam asked him who had said it. "Father Fitzgibbon," says Martin. "And did anything else happen at Mass this morning?" Mam persisted. "No, nothing at all," says Martin. "You weren't at Mass at all," Mam said. "The whole chapel had to be evacuated this morning right in the middle of Mass and you would have known about it if you had been there!"'

His religious observance notwithstanding, Martin was undeterred and he continued to travel to race meetings every weekend. He experienced the usual bumps and scrapes of a motocrosser. In 1993 he suffered his most serious injury at an international schoolboy motocross meeting in Naas, County Kildare, where he broke his ankle and wrist in a heavy fall.

Martin riding his first motorbike in the fields in Lusk.

None of this ever slowed Martin down and his ability to ride a motorbike very fast brought its rewards in dozens of race wins and several championships including the 1994 Schoolboy Southern Centre (of the Motor Cycle Union of Ireland) Junior Motocross title and the Grade C motocross and grass track championships in 1996. Martin continued to race on the dirt right up until he began tarmac racing and for a while he even combined the two disciplines.

The dirt bike racing honed Martin's skill on the slippery surfaces and big jumps that are a feature of the sport and many see this as the foundation of the breathtaking style he would later display on the roads. But Martin retained much more from his motocross years. From a very young age he was at ease on two wheels and was part of a racing scene that involved the close-knit Finnegan family who were to remain the bedrock of his support throughout his racing career.

Others, like Tony Carton, were very impressed by the youngster's dedication and determination to succeed. 'One day Martin appeared with some T-shirts that he had designed himself,' Tony recalls. 'They had a picture of him racing his motocross bike on the back and on the front he had "Round Tower Racing" printed. He was only about fourteen but even then he was thinking about how he should present himself and how he could get his sponsor a mention. Martin always had that great attention to detail.'

In his mid-teens, with a great deal already achieved in motocross, Martin began to display an interest in the branch of the sport that would eventually make him a household name.

Although Martin had used the workshops at Round Tower Plant to work on his motocross bikes, Tony's premises were also a place steeped in road racing. Almost inevitably Martin was drawn into the road racing world he found there. As a competitor himself Tony enjoyed the friendship of many other road racers who would call at the yard or fettle bikes in the workshop, and he sponsored another local man, Francis Everard, on the roads. Martin would go along with Francis and his mechanic, Lorcan McGuinness, to the races.

'Martin was always wanting to warm up the bike and bring it up to the line for us if we would let him,' Lorcan smiles. 'He was mad to have a go himself.'

One Monday morning in October 1996 Martin's mother lifted a pair of his jeans from the bedroom floor to put them into the wash. A small card fell from one of the pockets. 'I picked it up and I noticed that it had a lot of numbers on it and Martin's

With Tony Carton at the Manx Grand Prix in 2000.

name,' Margaret recalls. 'I took it into Jim and asked him what it was and he said "It looks like Martin was racing yesterday – this is his race licence."'

It was Martin's lap card from a Mondello Park track day where he had ridden Francis Everard's Yamaha on the previous Saturday.

Within a week Martin Finnegan was back at Mondello to compete in his first race on the black stuff.

Flying high during his motocross years.

1996
The first race

'Martin did over ninety laps, just stopping for fuel. We couldn't get him off the bike!' Lorcan McGuinness, Martin's first mechanic, recalls of that track day at Mondello in 1996. 'There was a guy there on a Honda Blackbird road bike and Martin chased him on the 250 until he got past and then the fella tried to stay with Martin. The guy ended up falling off the Blackbird! As soon as we came home Martin put in his entry for the Clubman's race meeting the following Sunday and off

we went. That was the start of it all.'

With no gear of his own Martin borrowed Francis Everard's helmet and Tony Carton's leathers and boots. 'He was as keen as mustard, he just couldn't wait to get started,' laughs Lorcan.

It wasn't an ideal debut for Martin as the heavens opened on the County Kildare circuit but he splashed around to take seventh and eighth positions in the two races.

With the spray flying off the back tyre, Martin splashes through the puddles during his first ever tarmac race at Mondello Park in October 1996.

In 1997 Martin combined dirt and tarmac racing, torn between his established success in motocross and his new passion for the short circuits.

'He'd be knocking at my bedroom window at 5 o'clock in the morning to get me up so we could get on the road,' Lorcan recalls. 'We'd travel to a motocross meeting in the North on a Saturday and then be at Mondello for a race on Sunday.'

With most of the short circuits – Aghadowey, Bishopscourt, Nutt's Corner and Kirkistown – in the North and motocross events in every corner of the country, Martin and Lorcan clocked up a lot of miles. 'Martin did his share of driving the van – even though he hadn't a licence!' Lorcan laughs.

As runner-up in the Southern Centre Grade B grasstrack championship Martin still tasted plenty of success off-road but he was also being noticed on the tarmac. 'Davy Wood [Joey Dunlop's manager and the leading figure in bike racing in the North at the time] asked me one day, "Who's this Finnegan fella then?"' Lorcan recalls. 'Davy had his eye on Martin even then.'

1997
'Who's this Finnegan fella then?'

ABOVE LEFT
In 1997 Martin continued to share the 250cc Yamaha with Francis Everard (standing beside Martin). Francis was an experienced road racer and Martin would go with the team to give a helping hand. Eventually Martin was to race under the direction of his former team-mate when Francis became Clerk of the Course at the Skerries and Killalane races.

LEFT
The Yamaha was repainted orange and black for 1997 but Martin still continued to race in borrowed helmet and leathers.

1998

On to the roads

Eighteen years old and Martin is pictured with the first trophy he won at a closed public road event – the West Cork hill climb in July 1998. He won Class C on his 250cc Honda.

OPPOSITE: Martin sits on the grid at Killalane on Sunday 13 September 1998 waiting to start his first ever road race. He is flanked by Lorcan McGuinness (in black), his first mechanic, and his sponsor and employer Tony Carton. Martin finished third in the 250cc Support race.

In 1998 Martin made two major decisions that would change the course of his motorcycling career. The first was his decision to give up his flourishing motocross career to concentrate on tarmac racing. It wasn't an easy choice as he had had the offer of top Suzuki machinery for the new season but his mind was made up about making the switch. As he said at the time, 'To be honest, I enjoyed my time in motocross but as soon as I started doing short circuits I got the tarmac bug.'

An ex-Gary Dynes 250cc Honda was purchased to replace the trusty Yamaha for a full season of racing in the 400cc Clubman's short-circuit championship. But the seventeen-year-old now had designs on another area of the sport – racing between the hedges on closed public roads.

In July Martin travelled with Tony Carton and fellow racers Maurice Wilson and his son Ian to County Cork to compete in a hill climb at Clonakilty. Martin had instant success, winning his class.

'By 1998 Martin was mad to have a go on the roads,' Tony remembers. 'I had raced the roads myself and I warned him that if he ever went on to the roads he'd never want to go back to the tracks. And that is exactly what happened.'

This new interest was hardly surprising given that Martin lived within earshot of the Skerries and Killalane circuits but it was to be the cause of great concern in the Finnegan household. When Martin announced that he intended to ride in his first road race at Killalane in September 1998 the family were caught up in a dilemma that many bike racers' families have had to face.

'We knew how dangerous road racing was and most of us didn't want Martin to go,' Martin's sister Geraldine says. 'He was very determined and he wasn't asking our permission. It was Daddy who intervened in the end.'

'I never asked Martin not to race. I knew that when he had his mind made up about doing something he'd do it,' his father Jim says. 'I just didn't want him going out there to race thinking that we were all against him. If we were with him it was one less thing that he would have to worry about and so I felt that we should all get behind him and support him.'

His knee skimming the kerb, Martin is inch-perfect through Ireland's Bend on the Round Tower Suzuki during the 2003 Ulster Grand Prix. He scored three sixth places in the Superbike, Supersport and 1000cc Production races with an eighth in the 600cc Production event, making it the most successful international road race performance of his career to date.

Martin gets all crossed up at Rhencullen during the 600cc Production TT in 2003. Although this area of the course was bathed in bright sunshine, the Mountain section was shrouded in mist. The deteriorating weather forced the race distance to be cut. Martin, who had climbed into fourth spot early in the race, dropped back into seventh place as he battled through the fog. Rhencullen was one of Martin's favourite sections of the course and when he built his own house in Lusk he named it after the famous jump.

TT starter Andy Fearn places his hands on the shoulders of Martin Finnegan and Adrian Archibald as they wait to start practice at the 2003 TT. Always trying to improve, Martin tried to get out to the front of the queue for every practice session – the fastest riders would come past during the lap and he could then follow them to learn the best lines around the course.

Martin gets the thumbs up from spectators at the Gooseneck as he wrestles his Round Tower Yamaha past their feet during the Supersport TT in 2003. Martin was well-built and very strong, making it easy for him to muscle a bike around on the road. His motocross experience gave him a natural feel for a bike's movement that his power allowed him to harness into an aggressive style. 2003 was the year when the fans really began to notice his all-action approach and they loved it.

If Martin Finnegan had one obsession it was drinking water! You rarely ever saw him without a bottle of the stuff in his hand and he would offer unprompted lectures on its purifying qualities and restorative powers. He told me once that he could drink a gallon a day when he was training or racing.

Martin wheelies the Round Tower Suzuki down Gillies Leap on his way to victory in the feature race at Skerries in 2003. This win on his home course thrust Martin into the Irish limelight as a massive local hero. For the faithful the promise was being realised, for the uncommitted there was a new Southern rider who could beat the hitherto dominant Northern riders. Not since Eddie Laycock in the late 80s had there been a rider from south of the border who could achieve that. Young and charismatic, Martin's popularity was to have a major impact on road racing in the south of Ireland during his career. The appearance of new road races in the South coincided with Martin's rise to prominence and the crowds who attended these new meetings included many Finnegan fans.

In a classic Irish road racing scene, Martin chases Richard Britton down a narrow lane between telegraph poles and hedges into Schoolhouse Corner during the Killalane Open race in 2003. It was the end of a domestic season for Martin in which he was dicing every weekend for race wins with the established frontrunners like Richard but it was a season that might not have been at all. At the beginning of the year an electrical fault had started a smouldering fire on one of the bikes in Martin's garage. His mother Margaret had discovered the blaze and her swift intervention had saved the bikes.

Pulling a massive wheelie, Martin celebrates winning the feature race at Killalane in 2003. In our first meeting at the beginning of the season Martin had asked me about getting more media coverage for his racing efforts and we had worked together throughout the year to ensure that his picture was appearing in racing magazines. Martin understood what made a good picture and I always ensured that he knew where I was on a race course for the slowing-down lap celebrations. Occasionally, we both ran foul of the race authorities over our desire to create a little exuberance like this. Although we enjoyed moments such as these, it was the images of Martin fully committed at the height of a race battle that were the real winners.

Threading the needle. Martin steers the ETi Ducati through the armco-lined streets of Macau during his first visit to the Chinese street race in November 2003. It was a baptism of fire for Martin as he struggled to get to grips with the unfamiliar Ducati machine and the Macau circuit. The annual event held at the end of the racing season is often seen as a holiday race but Martin approached it in his usual determined and professional manner. He had a special pair of leathers made combining the Eti and Round Tower branding and he had maintained his training schedule throughout the winter in preparation. His first Macau was a less successful foreign venture than his September trip to Frohburg in Germany had been, where he won two races, his only race victories outside Ireland and the Isle of Man. Nevertheless, Martin was to return to Macau every year for the rest of his career.

A picture of misery, Martin slumps against the tyre wall at San Francisco Bend to watch the remaining action in the Macau Grand Prix after he was forced to retire from the race on the third lap with a broken chain. Brushing against the walls of the narrow Macau circuit had left black marks on the shoulders of his leathers, an indication of how hard he had been riding.

Martin skims the kerb on his way to a double Superbike victory and a new outright lap record at Athea road races in County Limerick on the Danfay R1 Yamaha in June 2004.

Danfay
2004

The Yamaha R1 was the bike to have for the 2004 season and negotiations began in the early winter between the Finnegan camp and the Irish Yamaha importers Danfay, which eventually led to the creation of the Danfay/Round Tower race team for the new campaign.

For the opening race at Cookstown Martin appeared in what was to be his coolest ever livery, a blue and white design that retained his trademark logos and gave them a new and stylish flair.

Nor was it all just style. Martin's continuing progress was reflected in the early season results. He won the Open race at Cookstown before notching up an important milestone, his first International road race podium at the North West 200 in May.

By the end of the season Martin's skill had secured an Irish championship and his personal popularity saw him win the coveted Irish Motorcyclist of the Year title. He had achieved his first goal in racing – to be the number one road racer in Ireland – but with the success came new pressures.

His flamboyant riding style attracted huge attention and Martin became ever more exuberant as his confidence was boosted by his new-found fame. The fans loved the way Martin backed his bike into corners with the smoke billowing from the back tyre and the huge air he caught off the big jumps. But, at times, this could inhibit Martin's smoothness, costing him precious seconds as he fought against his bike rather than flowing with it. If his race results were affected, it would have a psychological impact as well. 'Martin thrived on success and when it didn't come his head dropped,' says Paul Phillips, who was working closely with Martin at the time. 'It was a side of him that was never seen in public but privately it was a very different story.'

Given that he was raised within the shadow of a round tower, it is hardly
surprising that Round Tower became a name synonymous with Martin

Martin cranks the Danfay Yamaha through the final bend ahead of Adrian Archibald's TAS Suzuki to secure his first international road race podium in the 2004 North West 200 feature race.

After the success of the North West 200, a lot was expected of Martin's 2004 TT campaign. A good practice week performance saw him on the leader board for all of the races but the opening Superbike TT brought a disappointment that was to set the tone for the remainder of the week. Captured here literally flying through Union Mills on the R1 Yamaha, Martin ground to a halt a lap later at the Verandah with a broken crankshaft. He also failed to finish the Superstock or 400cc races. Fourteenth place was the best he could do in the Production 600cc race and although he improved to sixth in the Supersport 600cc race, Martin ended the week with a fifth place on the Superstock-spec engined R1 in the Senior TT. For Martin the TT was now the pinnacle of his season and he had hoped to secure at least a podium finish. With his hopes dashed it was a weary trip back to Ireland to resume the rest of the year's racing.

Total concentration as Martin positions a sticker on the front of his R1.

Working among his mother's flower beds, Martin prepares his R1 Yamaha at the back of his parents' house. At this stage of his career Martin was still building his machines himself in Lusk, working at night or during time off from his day job at Tony Carton's. With two 600s, the Superstock and Superbike to build and maintain, Martin rarely left the garage between races once the season had started.

Nothing was left to chance as Martin checked and double-checked every nut and bolt, every cable and hose, during the preparation of his Yamahas. After all, his very life depended upon it.

2004 saw the beginning of one of the greatest rivalries in Irish road racing as Martin went head to head with Ryan Farquhar every weekend. Along with Richard Britton and Adrian Archibald, Ryan was one of the established stars of the sport and Martin's arrival on the scene began to shift the balance of power.

'Martin was coming through the ranks to challenge Richard, Adrian and me,' Ryan says. 'His goals were the same as mine – we wanted to win as many National road races in Ireland as we could and we both wanted a TT win.'

Right from the start of the season Ryan, from Killyman in County Tyrone, felt the heat of the exhausts of his County Dublin opponent and their rivalry was given extra spice by the North–South dimension. The fans loved their wheel-to-wheel tussles between the Irish hedges and everyone had their favourite.

'The way I saw it was that Martin was there to take my wages every week and I was trying to do the same to him,' Ryan laughs. 'We had to be at the top of our game to keep each other at bay.'

Although they didn't always see eye to eye off the track, they had a huge mutual respect for each other's ability on the bikes. 'I could have raced with Martin all day every day,' Ryan says. 'We never had a problem riding an inch from each other's back wheels.'

Although both men shared a very similar approach to racing, there was rarely any meeting of minds between Martin and Ryan once the helmets were taken off.

Martin closes in on Ryan during an epic battle over the big jumps at Dundalk in September 2004.

In motorcycle racing a huge amount of time is spent talking about tyres, as riders agonise over choosing the right rubber for the road conditions. When I watched Martin Finnegan in full flight I often wondered what all the debate and head scratching was about as it seemed that he rarely kept much rubber on the road at all! In this shot, taken at Fenton's Jump at the Mid Antrim road races in July, neither Martin nor Ray Porter have any contact with the tarmac. Watching through my lens, I saw Martin pull out of Ray's slipstream and move alongside him on the narrow stretch of road that is the start and finish straight at the Mid Antrim. I knew instantly that something special was about to happen as I tracked the pair of them hammering down the hill, side by side. Neither man was giving an inch in a high-speed game of bluff that could have ended in disaster. At the last, critical moment Ray blinked first as he rolled off his throttle – it was obvious that Martin had no intention of backing off. Squeezing the shutter just as they hit the crest of the jump, I silently prayed that I had captured the moment. And that it would be sharp.

Happy and relaxed in the morning sunshine, Martin pulls on his leathers to begin practice for the 2004 Macau Grand Prix.

The sun casts long shadows as it rises between the Macau skyscrapers during the opening early morning practice.

Keeping clear of the yellow walls, Martin steers the R1 through the twisty hill section of the Guia circuit.

Martin shows a healthy respect for the Macau armco as he negotiates the Solitude Esses on the Danfay Yamaha.

Enjoying a fun moment on a minimoto bike,
Martin launches the Enkalon Irish Motorcyclist
of the Year competition in 2005.

Martin is congratulated on winning the 2004 Enkalon Irish Motorcyclist of the Year
by Kim and Zoe Herron, the daughters of the late Tom Herron, who had been the
first winner of the prestigious award in 1978. The poll, voted for by the public, had
seen Martin pip Ryan Farquhar to the title, highlighting his huge popularity.

Champion

In 2004 the Irish Senior road race championship was decided on the final weekend of the season at Killalane. Martin was firmly focused on trying to win the title from his arch-rival, Ryan Farquhar. But he knew that he couldn't do it alone. Even if Martin won the race, second spot would be sufficient to give Ryan the championship. Martin needed a victory but he also needed someone to finish between himself and Ryan and he looked to his best friend in racing, Richard Britton, for that favour. The whole week leading up to the race was full of excitement and tension as he planned his strategy and prepared himself for the battle. On home turf, Martin was expected to deliver.

Hard at work in the garage, Martin prepares his bikes for the big race.

Martin's racing
leathers hang
between bicycle
wheels and
exhaust pipes on
the garage wall.

Taking a break from
his preparations,
Martin and his
brother Sean share a
Finnegan family tea
with their parents
Margaret and Jim.

In a moment of light-hearted banter among his closest racing friends, Martin is offered a sausage by Trevor Harbison as he chats with Richard Britton, Uel Duncan and Guy Martin on the morning of the race.

Helmet already on,
Martin walks to the line.

Never a fan of racing in the wet,
Martin notices the clouds closing in
over Killalane. Thankfully the rain
didn't fall until after the main race.

Nerves take their toll, forcing a
last-minute toilet break in the
cabbage field beside the grid.

The tension is obvious in Martin's eyes as his visor gets a final clean before the flag drops.

Setting off on a sighting lap.

Martin takes the chequered flag as Richard Britton follows him home in the all-important second place ahead of Ryan Farquhar. The result ensured that Martin won the Irish championship in the final race of the season.

Back in the paddock, everyone wants to shake the hand of the new champion.

The biggest hug came from Martin's proud father, Jim.

To the victor the spoils.

Vitrans
2005

It is often said that you should never go back in life, never cover the same ground twice, but in 2005 Martin Finnegan decided to return to the scene of his 2001 trials and tribulations, the British championship paddocks.

Determined to continue with the progress of 2004, his loyal Round Tower backers provided the funding for Martin to join the Vitrans Honda squad run by Scotsman Robbie Burns. The team ran top-class machinery using engines tuned in the famous Ten Kate workshop in Holland. With his bikes being prepared by the Vitrans mechanics, Martin, for the first time in his career, would be riding machines that he didn't have to build himself. He would simply have to train and turn up every weekend to race. To all intents and purposes, Martin was now a professional racer.

Scheduled to compete in the British Superstock championship, Martin would enjoy plenty of track time that would allow him to build his race speed and develop the bikes for the roads campaign ahead. Everything was concentrated on getting good results at the main international road meetings and, in particular, in pursuing that first Isle of Man TT victory. By now this had become the focus of Martin's road racing and by taking his racing effort to a new level he hoped to realise his dream. Unfortunately for his Irish fans it would also mean less racing on the home roads as the Vitrans deal only included a few local meetings. The plan was to bear rich fruit as his 2005 results were to be the best of Martin's racing career but it was also to be a year that would bring other life-changing events.

Powering the Vitrans Honda Fireblade over Black Hill during the North West 200 in May 2005.

Martin sits in the garage at Oulton Park waiting for a Superstock practice session to begin. His racing had taken on a new focus as he sharpened his skills for the highly competitive series. Vitrans team manager Joe Barr doubled as Martin's personal trainer and Joe devised a gruelling regime to improve Martin's fitness and build his stamina. Martin fought a constant battle with his weight throughout his career. It could fluctuate by as much as two stone depending on whether or not he was training and this had a major effect on his fitness level. Under Joe's expert guidance in 2005 he maintained a fitter and leaner physique.

With the Vitrans team came a whole new infrastructure for Martin's racing – mobile workshops, transporters, hospitality units, mechanics – all a far cry from building his own bikes and running his race team from his own lorry each weekend. He may have been up against faster opposition but Martin relaxed into the new set-up. 'He wasn't at BSB to win races,' his mechanic Gary Arnold says. 'Martin wanted to race on the tracks so that he could get his bikes set up properly and to build his speed and fitness through all the extra track time. In Ireland he had four or five laps of practice at the road races and then it was into the race. At the tracks there were two 45 minute practice sessions and then a half-hour race every weekend and Martin was racing against faster opposition that pulled him along.'

Martin wheelies the Vitrans Superstock Honda Fireblade out of Druid's corner at Oulton Park during the May Day meeting. He had immediately struck up a rapport with his new team-mate in the squad, John Laverty. 'Martin was great craic and he rode well within himself on the tracks as his heart lay elsewhere,' John remembers. 'He used to talk about going back to the "real racing" and I think he struggled with the circuits because he wasn't used to the idea that you could ride to the edge, fall off and get up to race again. He had been on the roads too long to change to that way of thinking.'

With the helicopter right on their tails, Ryan and Martin race elbow to elbow down the runway. At the last second the pair separated on either side of me and the helicopter blasted over my head – Martin said that it was the best day's fun he had ever had on the bike when he wasn't racing!

Intense rivals on the track, Ryan and Martin enjoyed every moment of the day at Ballykelly. Like every road racer I have ever met, they were both incredibly generous with their time and talent in the pursuit of what they knew would be a good photograph.

With the helicopter's skid just a few feet from his head, Martin pulls a wheelie at over 100mph as they race down the Ballykelly runway.

I was trying to think of a way to get a different, eye-catching picture in the run-up to the North West 200 in May 2005. As the race itself is so much about straight-line speed I came up with the idea of having a speed-testing session between Ireland's two top road racers, Martin Finnegan and Ryan Farquhar, and a helicopter. Finding a helicopter seemed like the only problem but it turned out to be quite easily resolved as a very kind Major in the British Army press office agreed to lend me a

Lynx helicopter, their two best pilots, a radio operator and the Ballykelly airbase in County Londonderry for the day! In glorious sunshine, Martin and Ryan raced the helicopter up and down the runway with the rotors only a few feet from their helmets. I told the riders what I wanted them to do, the man on the radio told the pilots what we intended and the skill of the four men, two on the ground and two in the air, brought everything together for my lens.

Mr TT! A delighted Martin poses with his
first TT garland under the podium.

'How was it for you?' Martin and Adrian Archibald exchange stories
of their race as they walk towards the podium. After six laps of a
Superbike TT there are always tales to tell and although Martin
seemed slightly overwhelmed by his first visit to a TT winners'
enclosure, he relaxed on his way up to the rostrum.

A fly for every mile.

It was all smiles in the Superbike TT
winners' enclosure as Martin is
congratulated on his third-place finish
by Adrian Archibald (second) and John
McGuinness (winner). The focus of
Martin's plans for 2005 were on TT
success and they brought immediate
results in the opening race of the week.

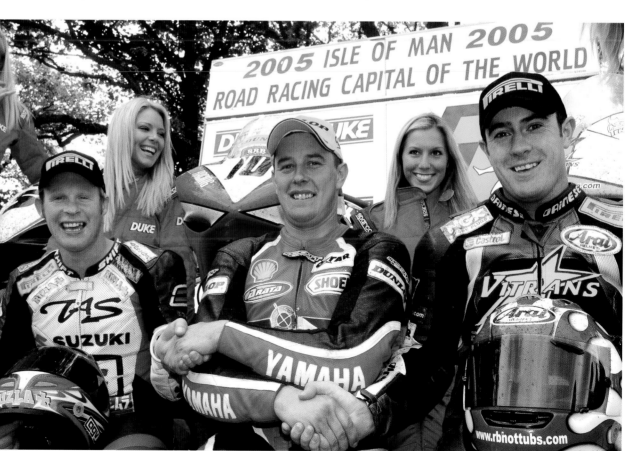

Displaying the style over Ballaugh Bridge that brought him his first TT podium, Martin was to become almost as famous for his exploits over the humpback bridge as for any of his other TT achievements. During practice sessions the marshals, who could see Martin approaching on the other side of the bridge, would blow their whistles to signal his much anticipated arrival. Hearing the whistles, the waiting fans in Ballaugh village blasted air horns, waved Irish flags and broke into cheers as Martin leapt the bridge in spectacular style.

Enjoying what was to be his finest hour in motorcycle racing, Martin jokes with Adrian Archibald and John McGuinness on the Superbike TT podium as he relives a close encounter for his rivals. Martin was to have an even closer encounter with John during Friday's Senior TT. 'I had seen my pit boards and I knew that I had the race won,' John remembers. 'I was cruising home over the Mountain when Martin came flying past me at the Bungalow, scratching like mad. He was battling for the final podium spot and he was on a mission. It took me by surprise and I nearly jumped out of my skin but the cheeky bugger told me after the race that I had got in his way!' Martin's efforts were to be in vain as two slow pit stops had cost him too much time and he eventually lost out on a second podium place by less than a second to his former TT mechanic and good friend, Guy Martin. Despite his personal disappointment, Martin stopped his bike outside the winners' enclosure where Guy was celebrating and went in to offer his own congratulations.

Hand-painted in traditional fashion, the vintage TT scoreboard displays the details of Martin's incredible final lap of the Senior TT in 2005. Riding number 4, Martin completed the sixth lap of the race in 17 minutes, 49.39 seconds at a speed of 127.014mph to become the fastest Irishman ever, and the third fastest man of all time, around the famous Mountain circuit. His average speed for the whole race was 123.302mph.

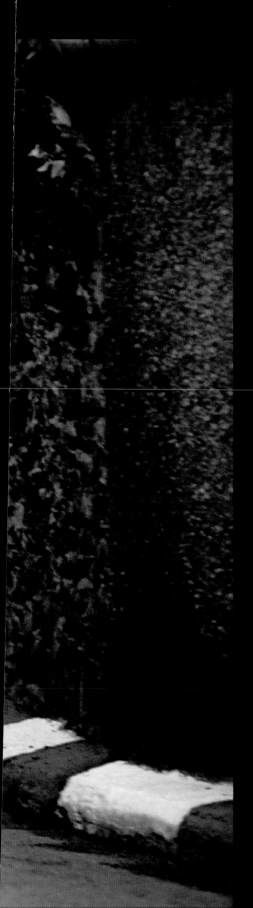

I took this picture of Martin at the bottom of Barregarrow during the final session of 2005 TT practice. Far faster than anyone else down through the notoriously bumpy bend, Martin kept the throttle pinned against the stop as he jumped off the first rise and landed in the hollow where his Vitrans Honda bottomed out completely. The fibreglass of the fairing was ground to dust against the tarmac. Many people who look at the picture think that the bike is broken or that Martin is actually starting to crash but this is the way he rode the bend on every lap. Martin had the muscle and skill to control a 200bhp Superbike at these extremes like no other rider of his generation.

Knowing I had captured something special, I wired the picture to the newspapers and magazines that Friday evening. On Monday morning I received a phone call from Gary Pinchin, the sports editor of *Motorcycle News*. 'What the hell is going on in this picture of Finnegan?' Gary asked, not quite believing me when I told him that Martin took Barregarrow like this on every lap. When *MCN* appeared on Wednesday morning the picture was printed across two pages and the story talked about how the TT took man and machine to the very edge of what was possible on two wheels. Four TT races had elapsed in the days in between this picture being taken and *MCN*'s publication and Martin had won none of them. Nevertheless, he was now receiving the biggest headlines.

By the end of TT race week, Martin had made his mark on the results sheet but he had left an even greater impression with his spectacularly exciting riding style, a style that some commentators christened 'controlled hairiness'.

Martin sweeps the Vitrans
Supersport Honda onto the
Mountain Mile during practice
for the 2005 Isle of Man TT.

Martin also raced in some selected Irish road races in 2005, returning to his grassroots after the hospitality units and grid girls of the BSB scene. In May the huge Vitrans transporter rolled into the Tandragee paddock, which had turned into a quagmire after a week of heavy rain. The team mechanics had to wheel the bikes through liquid mud to the start line, bringing buckets of water and sponges to wash down the wheels before they put on the tyre warmers. For some of the Vitrans squad this introduction to Irish road racing was a baptism of fire, but for Martin and Richard Britton it wasn't anything that they hadn't seen before and they took it all in their stride.

The little lanes that make up the Irish road courses are a million miles from the wide open spaces of Donington Park or Silverstone. In some places, like here on the Skerries back road, the tarmac is only twelve feet wide. Although he struggled to adapt to the short circuits, Martin was in his element fighting his Honda's front wheel out of the grass on Gillies Leap and hurtling between these hedges at 150mph.

Martin struggles to carry home his haul of trophies.

Finnegan-mania struck the Skerries paddock after his hat trick of wins. Martin sold two thousand T-shirts over the weekend.

Releasing the tension with the bubbly on the Skerries podium.

Martin's return to Skerries 100 in July 2005 marked the highest point of his career on the Irish roads. In front of hordes of partisan fans he scored a treble, notching up wins in the 600cc, Open and Grand Final races, and unleashing a wave of Finnegan-mania in the paddock and around the course. Martin soaked up the adulation, his confidence boosted by all of the attention he received. Everyone expected him to produce the goods in his home races and Martin felt under enormous pressure to perform. Always conscious of how he was regarded, he wanted to please his huge following of Irish fans and at Skerries in 2005 there were a lot of very happy Finnegan followers.

Martin delights the fans at Dukes' Bends as he hauls the Vitrans Fireblade through the S-bend with the front wheel skimming the road.

2005 was to become an even more momentous year for Martin and his fiancée Brenda with the birth of their daughter Rachel in June. The couple had been together since 2001. 'When we met at first I didn't know who Martin was or what he did. When I visited his house and saw all of the trophies I asked him "Is there someone who lives here who is really good at something?"' Brenda laughs as she remembers. Unfazed, Martin continued his persistent pursuit and within six months the pair were an item. A year later they had set up home together. 'Although I never really got involved in the bike racing scene with Martin we had a great time together doing other crazy stuff like skydiving, white-water rafting and bungee jumping,' Brenda says. 'We skied together every year and pushed each other all the time. We were both really competitive and it was part of the attraction that brought us together.' They were engaged after Martin proposed on Christmas morning in 2004.

The coveted TT replica trophies are lined up on the kitchen windowsill in the Finnegan home, a daily reminder of what had been achieved and the ultimate goal still sought.

Brenda, Rachel and Martin in the kitchen of their new home in Lusk.

The gathered gallery watches at Quarry Bends as Martin kicks up the spray on the final lap of the Supersport race at Dundrod. Never fond of racing in the wet as he didn't enjoy riding in close proximity to other riders in the rain, Martin broke away from the pursuing pack and rode a lonely race to secure second spot.

Martin's season drew to a successful close as he completed a treble of podiums in all of the international road races with second place in the Supersport race at the Ulster Grand Prix. The race was won by 600cc specialist Ryan Farquhar, as new kid on the block Cameron Donald ran in third. Martin's previous podiums at the North West 200 and the Isle of Man TT had come on 1000cc machines which were more suited to his build and weight, distinct disadvantages on the lighter 600cc bikes on which Martin often struggled. Martin stood all of these rules on their head at Dundrod with a brilliant second spot against riders like Donald, John McGuinness, Richard Britton, Jason Griffiths and Adrian Archibald.

Martin may have enjoyed the adulation of the crowd after winning races on summer Sundays but by winter Mondays he was back to his job servicing plant equipment. After serving his apprenticeship as a teenager with the Irish railway company CIE, Martin had returned to Lusk to work for Tony Carton. As a dedicated supporter of Martin's, Tony understood the need for Martin to devote time to his racing if he was to continue to progress. During the summer months Tony allowed him to take time off to train and race and he continued to pay Martin's salary. In return, Martin returned to full-time work when the racing season ended.

Another job finished, Martin gathers up his tools and heads for home.

Martin travelled around the countryside, working on machinery in all weathers.

At times it meant getting down into the midst of the dirt to carry out the work.

Martin checks if everything is running properly before heading to the next job.

2005 was a year of very mixed emotions for Martin. On the race track he had moved to the next level, riding in a professional team and improving his results on the big stage. Along the way he had taken a big step closer to his ultimate goal, a TT win. At home new responsibilities had arrived with the birth of his daughter Rachel. As doting a Dad as could be imagined, Martin revelled in the new-found joy of fatherhood and he completed the building of a new home in Lusk for his family.

Just as everything seemed to be falling into a happy rhythm in Martin's life, that rhythm was shattered by the death of his closest friend in racing, Richard Britton. Competing against each other every weekend, the pair had become constant companions and they were together in Ballybunnion in County Kerry on Sunday 18 September when Richard crashed after his bike seized in the 250cc race. Martin was riding behind Richard when the accident happened. He stopped and ran back to offer assistance but there was nothing he could do to help his friend hold on to life.

Martin and Rachel relax after feeding time.

In 2005 Richard Britton joined Martin in
the Vitrans team for the Ulster Grand Prix.

A bond broken

It was perhaps inevitable that Martin Finnegan and Richard Britton would become close friends, given their approachable and easy-going natures. Similar in size and physique, they mirrored each others' exciting riding styles. They also shared the same intense love of road racing. Brought together by the close-knit surroundings of the Irish paddocks, their friendship developed as they both moved to the front rank of their chosen sport.

Although sharing the same laid-back approach, Richard's refusal to take life too seriously tempered Martin's implacably determined focus. Where Martin would slump into dejection when he failed to win, Richard smiled and said there would be another day.

Martin hitches a lift back to the paddock with Richard after breaking down during practice for the Tandragee 100 in 2003.

Stephen Thompson, Martin and Richard had become known as the 'Three Amigos' around the paddock. 'We had got to know each other through racing together in Macau over the past few years and when we came home we would all be on the phone three or four times a week,' Stephen explains. 'We would keep in touch and help each other out, maybe picking up parts or delivering stuff to one another. We would always be there for each other and Martin and Richard were both really easy to get on with because they were so relaxed about everything.'

Distraught and grief-stricken following Richard's death in September 2005, Martin rang me on the evening before his friend's funeral. He asked if I could bring a copy of this photograph of the 'Three Amigos', which I had taken in Macau the year before, to the Britton home in Enniskillen the next morning. Martin placed the picture of the three friends inside Richard's coffin before the funeral procession made its way to the graveyard through the rain.

Klaffi
2006–7

Martin's excellent results had brought him to the notice of a new team towards the end of 2005. Former Austrian world sidecar champion Klaus Klaffenbock had become infatuated with achieving the same personal racing goal as Martin, a TT win, and for the 2006 season he wanted to bring his Klaffi World Superbike team to the Isle of Man. Martin was at the top of his list for a berth in the squad.

Naturally excited by the prospect of having WSB-series calibre machinery, with Honda factory support, Martin secured the deal in the autumn of 2005 and he had his first outing on the Klaffi bike at the Macau Grand Prix. Unfortunately the initial promise began to fade when it became obvious that the team was divided in its objectives and its resources were spread too thinly between the WSB effort and the road racing initiative.

At the same time Martin was battling personal demons that hindered his preparation. He had been badly affected by Richard Britton's death at the end of 2005 and his involvement in the establishment of a new business venture was placing intense demands upon his time. He found it difficult to find the time to train. Returning to a situation where he had to recruit and organise his own race team undermined Martin's ability to fulfil the huge expectations that confronted him. Only victory at the highest level would be sufficient for himself and his fans now.

This combined lack of team and personal focus thwarted Martin's progress in 2006. While there were triumphs at Irish National level, culminating in victory in the Irish Superbike championship once again, Martin failed to advance on his tally of International road race podiums.

This raises the question why Martin opted to remain racing under the Klaffi banner for 2007. There were changes within the team that gave Martin a renewed confidence. The squad dropped out of World Superbike competition for the new season, allowing the Austrian outfit to have a greater concentration on pure road racing. He had also been offered a deal to race the Italian MV Agusta machines, bringing the factory back to road racing for the first time in over thirty years.

With the Klaffi deal limited to the international events in 2007, Martin was to compete in fewer Irish races. While he achieved solid performances at the TT, he again failed to advance on his 2005 results. By mid-season Martin had decided that he needed to move in a different direction and the partnership with Klaffi came to an end.

Wheelieing the Klaffi Honda Fireblade over
Ago's Leap in the 2007 Superbike TT.

Martin rang me up one morning in October 2005 and asked me if I was busy on Thursday. I said I didn't think so and asked him what was happening. 'I want you to go to Austria with me,' he laughed. 'I am signing for a new team.' We went to Austria on the Thursday, to Wels, where Klaus 'Klaffi' Klaffenbock had his workshops in a courtyard of lovely old farm buildings on the edge of town. Martin was really excited about joining the team and riding the same machines as Frankie Chili and Max Neukirchner had been racing in the World Superbike championship that season. He was very impressed by the Klaffi set-up at Wels, even slightly dazzled by the image that the team projected, as he swapped the number 7 on the legendary Chili's bike to his own 45 for the pictures. Unfortunately some of that early promise was to diminish when Klaus signed ex-MotoGP rider Alex Barros at the beginning of 2006. Barros was to spearhead the team's WSB campaign, concentrating the focus and resources of the Klaffi operation towards the WSB series. This would be at the expense of their road racing effort and it led to problems for Martin as the season progressed.

ABOVE: Martin and Klaus Klaffenbock pictured outside the Klaffi team workshop in Austria in October 2005.

RIGHT: Skirting the wall at Moorish Bend, Martin has his first outing on the Klaffi bike at the Macau Grand Prix in November 2005.

Martin had a victorious start on the Klaffi Honda in Ireland, winning the feature race at the Cookstown 100 in April 2006 and setting a new lap record along the way. In spite of his spectacular leaps over Cooley Hill at Tandragee the following month he could only manage second in both Open races behind new rival Cameron Donald. In the first half of the season the Klaffi bikes ran in a silver and grey paint scheme.

Joining the Klaffi team, with its World Superbike pedigree, earned Martin a seat at the top table of road racing. He joined Adrian Archibald, Ian Hutchinson, Ryan Farquhar, John McGuinness and Ian Lougher at Castle Rushen in the Isle of Man in January to launch the 2006 TT. Echoes of another gathering of men for a famous final meal seemed to surround the riders as they enjoyed their banquet.

Steering the Klaffi Honda between the walls of Guthries Bends, Martin climbs the mountain with Ramsey Bay in the background during evening practice for the Isle of Man TT in June. The bikes had undergone a colour change since the start of the season.

By 2006 Martin was riding more spectacularly than ever, leaping Ballaugh Bridge during the Supersport TT even higher than before. His race results suffered because of the machines, never because of his machine control. Some questioned whether he was riding on the very edge of, or perhaps even beyond, his limits but Martin had consummate belief in his own ability. I used to ask him after a race if he had had any 'moments' – racing parlance for near crashes or scary happenings – and Martin always replied in the same way: 'I never have moments, Stephen!'

Catching the evening sun on the Klaffi Honda Superbike, Martin begins the charge over the mountain during TT practice in 2006.

Looking pensive as he waits in the back of his transporter to begin a practice session, Martin faced a troubled TT in 2006. The Klaffi team was undermanned and the hard-pressed mechanics struggled to prepare all of the machines needed for a week of practice and another week of racing. They found it difficult to set up the more highly-strung and nervous-handling Klaffi bikes for the bumpy TT course and Martin complained that the Superbike's power was so unmanageable that it just wanted to wheelie everywhere. 'The bikes were essentially built for track racing and what works on the short circuits doesn't always work on the roads,' explains Martin's mechanic, Gary Arnold. 'We had difficulty adapting the suspension in particular.' Reliability was also an issue and in the end Martin's best finish was a fourth place in the Superbike TT.

Martin had also been deeply unsettled after witnessing a horrific accident at the beginning of practice week that involved his close friend, Seamus Greene. Jun Maeda was killed and Seamus, who had spannered for Martin during his first TT in 2002, was very badly injured when the Irish rider collided with the Japanese star at 160mph on Ballahutchin Hill. Jun had broken down and was touring slowly back to the paddock when Seamus, travelling much faster in the slipstream of another rider, had been unable to see him until it was too late. No matter how much belief a rider has in his own ability there are times when the circumstances are beyond even the finest racer's control. In the almost uncontrolled environment of a road race the consequences can be, and often are, horrendous.

Perhaps the only way that a road racer can deal with these dangers is to block them out completely. The 'it won't happen to me' mentality is the road racer's number one defence. Martin held that belief more strongly than anyone else I have ever met.

A lone spectator watches Martin climb the hill out
of the Gooseneck as the sun goes down on a 2006
TT evening practice session.

Martin is sitting on his 200bhp Klaffi Honda Superbike surrounded by a horde of similar machines on the grid at the start and finish straight at the Mid Antrim road races. A row of telegraph poles rise out of the grass verges which have been hastily cut back from the narrow strip of rolling tarmac. In a few moments the flag will drop and the screaming, jostling pack will hurtle down this road only a few inches apart into Fenton's Jump. Fenton's is a 120mph left-hander which is taken on the back wheel with the bike tipped over to the left to stop it from hammering straight on into the hedgerow. It is all a little different from the likes of Monza or Hockenheim where Messrs Barros, Chili and Neukirchner usually took the Klaffi Hondas to work.

A smiling Martin gives the V-for-victory as he celebrates his return to winning ways at Faugheen. Martin was a rider who thrived on success. It infused him with confidence and boosted his morale. 2006 had been bleak, with no wins since the start of the season at Cookstown but Faugheen was the beginning of a turnaround in his season that would see him take the Irish Open road race championship for the second time in his career.

Ray Porter looks on as Martin punches the air with joy as he crosses the line after doing the double in the Senior and Grand Final races at Faugheen in July 2006. His bike was fitted with a new engine specially built by Guy Martin and with the aid of new engine-management electronics, all of which Martin paid for himself, he had eventually made the Klaffi Honda rideable on the road courses.

Mick Kelly, a loyal Finnegan fan, sports a home-made banner in support of his man. In spite of his problems on the track in 2006–7 Martin remained as popular as ever with racing fans all over Ireland and abroad. The support he received was a vital component of his racing and he enjoyed the attention and limelight. Martin was always ready to take time to chat and sign autographs for fans, not just because it was part of his job, but because it was as important to him as it was for them.

When I showed Martin this picture we joked that it proved that road racers have a screw loose! It was taken at Fenton's Jump during the Open race at the Mid Antrim 150, where Martin scored a brilliant treble in 2006.

Cranked over and riding on only the edge of his back wheel, Martin exits Sam's Tunnel at over 130mph during the 600cc race at the Skerries 100 in 2006. When I went to this spot to photograph Martin he burst into view so breathtakingly fast and kicking up so much dust that I didn't think I would ever be able to get any pictures at all. Eventually I focused on a spot on the road and hoped that I would be able to freeze his crazy blur of noise and speed as he flew past.

Rachel doesn't look as if she wants to go for a lap on her Dad's bike at Walderstown road races in County Westmeath in July 2006 – maybe she had seen some of the photographs of his antics!

In a race scene more reminiscent of 1957 than 2007, Martin steers his bike through a tunnel of spectators at over 150mph during the Grand Final at Killalane in September. Having parted company with Klaffi, Martin's loyal Round Tower sponsors had helped him acquire a Yamaha R1 for what was to be his last race on the roads of southern Ireland.

Martin receives a silver replica from Robert Dunlop at the TT prizegiving in the Villa Marina in 2006. With the end of 125cc racing at the TT, Robert was no longer able to compete in the event and he was the guest of honour at the awards presentation. Sadly, both men were to lose their lives in race crashes within a fortnight of each other in May 2008.

The continuous progress that Martin had made on his way to the top level of road racing had seemed to falter during the Klaffi years. By the end of the 2007 season many people, who were unaware of the personal issues and machine troubles that he was dealing with, were beginning to question whether his best days in road racing had come and gone. Stung by such criticism and certain of his own ability, Martin was more determined than ever to achieve his goal of a TT win. All he needed was the machinery that could take him there.

Martin was all smiles with his new Italian MV Agusta machinery at the 2007 TT.

MV

MV Agusta is perhaps the most romantic name in motorcycle racing, conjuring up memories of legends like Hailwood and Agostini gliding to victory on the sleek red and silver machines. In 2007 Martin Finnegan joined that list of legends in a deal brokered by former Honda and Norton team boss Barry Symmons. In January 2007 Martin and Barry travelled to Varese to meet MV boss Claudio Castiglioni at the Italian factory. Martin made such an impression that by the time the pair were heading back to Ireland he had become the only Irish 'works' rider in MV Agusta history. 'That was always something that Martin was very, very proud of,' Barry remembers. Although its glorious history had faded into the dim and distant past, MV was rebuilding its business and wanted to increase the profile of the beautiful, new F4 machine through a racing campaign. Martin would spearhead their road racing efforts and his contract provided him with a pair of factory-built Superstock-spec F4s. The main ambition for everyone involved was a good finish in the Superstock Isle of Man TT.

Although many people doubted the MV's speed and above all its ability to last four laps of a gruelling Superstock TT race, Martin was convinced that it was good enough and he posted the second fastest time in practice. Had it not been for a huge front-end slide as he entered the village of Crosby at high speed during the race, Martin may well have achieved his ambition of putting the MV on the podium. His fourth place finish was a brilliant result, nonetheless, on a new and untried bike. The MV factory was delighted.

Martin in action on the MV Agusta at Creg Ny Baa during the 2007 Superstock TT race.

FAR LEFT: When Martin blasted the MV Agusta off the start line in the Open race at Tandragee in May 2007 it was the first time that a 'works' MV had taken to the roads in anger in thirty-five years. Not since the heyday of Giacomo Agostini had a factory-supported MV been raced between the hedges and Martin was leading the team's pure road racing renaissance. It was almost a fairytale return as Martin was pipped to the line for the race win by Cameron Donald (86, Honda) by the slender margin of a six thousandth of a second! A fortnight later Martin would have what he described as his 'scariest moment in racing' on a stationary MV when the clutch failed on the grid for the start of the North West 200 Superstock race. Martin, sitting on the second row, curled himself into a ball as he waited to be shunted from behind by the rest of the field as they blasted away. Thankfully, everyone avoided his stricken machine.

LEFT: The MV made a guest appearance on the happy occasion of Brenda and Martin's wedding in Lusk in November 2007.

ABOVE: Martin is oblivious to the sun sparkling on Ramsey Bay behind him as he brakes hard for Guthries Bends during an evening practice session at the 2007 Isle of Man TT.

Emerging from the winter shadows, Martin prepares for his first test on the JMF Millsport Yamahas at Kirkistown in February 2008.

The Final Lap

By the start of 2008 Martin was enjoying life to the full. The previous two years had not been as fruitful in racing as he might have hoped but there were other satisfactions and pleasures. He had settled into a comfortable life in the new home he shared with his beautiful wife and daughter in Lusk. His racing exploits had made Martin Finnegan a household name and helped him to establish a thriving motorcycle business. At twenty-eight years of age Martin had achieved much more in life than many men who had lived twice as long. Given the dangers of the sport and everything that he now had at stake, retirement from road racing may have seemed a possibility but there was still one piece of unfinished business.

'Martin said he wanted to keep going until he had won a TT,' his wife Brenda recalls. 'The TT win had become almost an obsession for him. It was no longer something that he just wanted by that stage, it had become a need and it was difficult for him to stop when he had worked so hard towards that goal.'

After the failings of the Klaffi years Martin didn't want to go back to running his own team with all the pressure and hassle that goes with it. He knew that he would need better machinery and a well-funded team supporting him if he hoped to fulfil his ambition. The offer of top-class Yamaha machinery from the JMF Millsport squad at the end of 2007 seemed to present Martin with the opportunity that he was looking for and he joined the team before Christmas. His early season performances in 2008 appeared to confirm the hope that Martin had found the bikes that could carry him to success in the Isle of Man.

Sadly that hope was to be cruelly destroyed in a fatal crash at the Tandragee 100 on 3 May 2008 that cost Martin his life.

Mechanics Martin Gallagher and Alistair Christie look on as Martin, meticulous as ever, lines up the decals on the front of his bike at Kirkistown in County Down in February.

The Kirkistown test was an important day for Martin. Although the JMF Millsport team was equipped with excellent machinery, Martin wanted to be sure that everything was as he wanted it to be. With electronics and suspension technicians in attendance he was able to get the bikes set up and he left the circuit very happy. 'We have a winner here' was Martin's verdict in a phone call to Tony Carton on his way home.

Back to his fighting weight and with real confidence in his bikes, Martin soaks up the winter sunshine at Kirkistown.

Enjoying a light-hearted moment as Martin is captured with his sample bottle in his hand during the test!

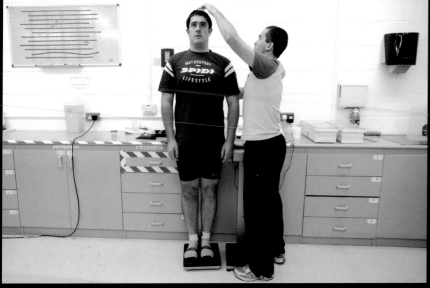

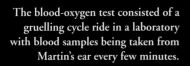

Having his height and weight recorded.

The blood-oxygen test consisted of a gruelling cycle ride in a laboratory with blood samples being taken from Martin's ear every few minutes.

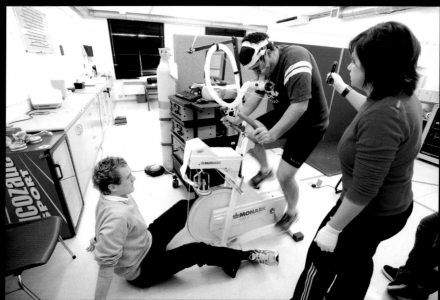

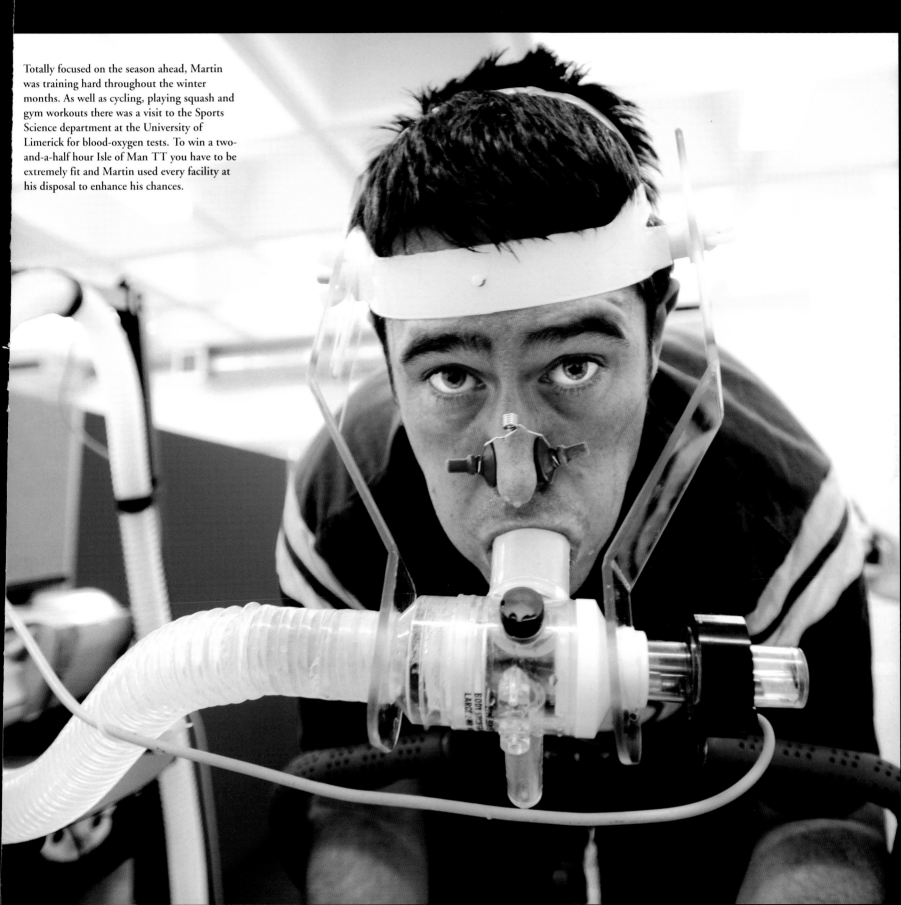

Totally focused on the season ahead, Martin was training hard throughout the winter months. As well as cycling, playing squash and gym workouts there was a visit to the Sports Science department at the University of Limerick for blood-oxygen tests. To win a two-and-a-half hour Isle of Man TT you have to be extremely fit and Martin used every facility at his disposal to enhance his chances.

Martin has both wheels off the ground at Black's Farm during the season opener at Cookstown in April 2008. Practice problems forced him to start in the second wave of both Superbike races and he battled through the pack to finish second behind Ryan Farquhar in each event.

Shaving the privets on the way into Mackney's corner . . .

. . . and skimming under the flag marshal's nose on the way out during the 600cc race at Cookstown. Martin finished in third place.

Powering out of Bell's Crossroads, Martin on his way to victory in what was to be his last race. It was the forty-third Irish National road race win of his career.

Tandragee was Martin's favourite Irish road race course and he arrived in County Armagh full of confidence after his performance at Cookstown the week before. Lined up alongside Keith Amor (24, Honda), Ryan Farquhar (77, Kawasaki) and Adrian Archibald (13, Suzuki), Martin got a good start in the first event of the day, the Open race. Martin was leading the race when it was red-flagged following a crash and he followed Ryan home in the restart to take overall victory in the two-part race.

Joking with Adrian Archibald and his mechanics on the grid, Martin was in great form at Tandragee. We had chatted about his picture being in that morning's paper and he was delighted that he was making headlines again. As I turned to leave the grid, Martin was pulling on his helmet to start the race.

'I was never so close to racing that it became my life, but I understood the pleasure that it could bring and never more so than at Tandragee in 2008. The weather was lovely during practice on Friday evening and it was great to be in the paddock with Martin and Rachel, surrounded by all the boys in the team. Things were going well for Martin, and I was chatting to people over a glass of wine as they drifted in and out of the awning. Everything was so easy-going and relaxed in the sunshine. Rachel was watching TV in the motorhome and when the practice session ended I went in to make Martin his favourite tea – chicken fajitas. We were there as a family and I was very, very happy.

When I woke up the next morning Martin and Rachel were already up. She was sitting on his knee and they were watching a film together as they ate a big bowl of porridge. I remember being so aware of how good things were as I stood there watching them. It felt that we had found our place in life, our niche, but road racing can have an awful flip side and you don't see it coming. I didn't. At times I had worried about things going wrong, but I didn't think about it at all that day. After a while Martin started to get ready to go, pulling on his leathers and boots. He lifted his helmet, kissed Rachel and me goodbye, and went out to race.

We never saw him again.'

BRENDA FINNEGAN

Martin pulls on his helmet for the final time on the grid at Tandragee.

These three, uncropped, photographs are the last frames I ever took of Martin Finnegan. They were captured at Cooley Hill on the first lap of his final race, the 600cc event at Tandragee. Perhaps appropriately, Martin jumped out of my frame in the final image.

A few moments later the race was red-flagged. I knew almost immediately that Martin
had been involved in an incident because he was the only rider who did not come past as
the rest made their way back to the paddock. A few minutes later a race marshal told me
that Martin had crashed at Marlacoo Corner.

Martin's bike lies smashed and broken on the bank at Marlacoo Corner where it came to rest following the crash on the second lap of the 600cc race. Approaching the bend at over 150mph Martin experienced a complete front brake failure. With typically lightning reactions, Martin responded by hammering the bike down through the gears and steering left instead of right as he attempted to give himself more space to slow down in. A skid mark, over 130 metres long, was evidence of his desperate battle to slow the Yamaha using only the back brake but he was still carrying too much speed when he reached the corner. Martin and the bike were flung into the bank at 100mph, killing him instantly.

Thousands of people lined the streets of Lusk and every space was filled around the village green as Martin's coffin was carried into the church during his funeral on 7 May. Martin was laid to rest in his racing leathers and his mother, Margaret, walked behind the coffin carrying his helmet.

'In some ways we didn't realise how popular Martin really was until that day,' his father Jim says. 'We are very very proud of all that Martin achieved but even if he had finished last in every race in the last ten years we have still lost our son now. When we look out the window, we don't think of Martin flying by on a bike, we miss him going past with Rachel by the hand.'

CHELSEA
A BACKPASS THROUGH HISTORY

Written by
Michael O'Neill

Danann
BOOKS

First Published by Danann Publishing Ltd

CAT NO: DAN0353

Photography courtesy of The Press Association & Getty Images,
Photoshot, UPPA, Talking Sport, Fotosports

Book layout & design Darren Grice at **Ctrl-d**

Made in EU.
ISBN: 978-1-9997050-0-8

THE CONTENTS

INTRODUCTION 4

THE FOOTBALL LEAGUE 6

IN THE BEGINNING 8

THE EARLY YEARS 10

THE POST WAR YEARS 20

THE DOCHERTY ERA 28

THE FA CUP AT LAST 36

THE FUTURE BEGINS 50

THE MIGHTY DUO 62

THE PLAYERS 76

THE MANAGERS 88

THE STATISTICS 96

INTRODUCTION

It is impossible to trace the exact origins of what evolved into the riveting sport known as football, the *"beautiful game"*; they are lost somewhere in the mists of memory that swirl around human activity as they may do on an autumn morning at Anfield. So we must indulge in that wonderful pastime, speculation, spiced with some good, calculated guesses.

Whenever football is mentioned, Britain will be part of the conversation before long, so it is fitting that Britain has its part in the ancient folklore of the origins of the sport.

Local legends in both Chester and Kingston-on-Thames tell us that a game was played in those towns in which the amputated head of a defeated Danish prince or ruffian, which probably came to the same thing, was kicked around. That seems to be a good starting point; considering the curses from the terraces that wish a similar fate would befall the top goal-scorers of opposing teams in the present-day game. In Derbyshire they would have us believe that Anglo-Saxon victory celebrations against the Romans brought on the desire to kick something else, as kicking the Romans had been such fun.

Long before that, written evidence supports the claim that the Romans and Greeks were instrumental in the game's birth. They played many ball games as the Roman writer Cicero testified. One unfortunate man was killed whilst having a shave, he wrote, when a ball came hurtling into the barber's shop where he was sitting. The Romans used ball games for more serious reasons, too. They were considered a good way to sharpen a soldier's reactions and spirit for battle.

The Chinese, inventive as they have always been, seem to have been ahead of the game as well. A form of football was played in the third and second centuries BC. during the Han dynasty, when people were already rushing around and kicking leather balls into a small net or through a hole in a piece of silk cloth stretched between two poles. It was probably played for the emperor's amusement. There is no record of what happened if he got bored and relegation would not have been much fun back then. The game, as played by Chinese aristocrats, was known as t'su chu. But the Aztecs, Persians, Vikings and Japanese all had some form of ball game for entertainment. Luckily not against one another.

It was the English peasants, however, who were responsible for the increasing popularity of the game sometime around the 9th century AD. This old football game was a real free-for-all and participants were allowed to bite, punch, stab and gouge as well as kick. Not much has changed in a thousand years after all. The ball had to be taken to a certain spot and this game proved to be so popular that fields would be overflowing with eager sports fans. As you can imagine, it often got wildly out of hand. Archers would even sneak away from archery practice to watch.

Medieval England was undoubtedly the place where football began its unstoppable campaign. There is an account of a match played in 1280. It took place in Northumberland near Ashington. It is also the first report of a player being killed when he ran onto the dagger worn by an opposing player. There is no report as to whether the dagger was in or out of the sheath at the time!

Incidents of violence became so frequent, in fact, that in 1365 King Edward the Third banned the game altogether. The ban was also an attempt to keep his archers at their practice (yes, they were still sneaking away from work) as their skills were sorely needed following the outbreak of the black plague that had decimated the population of the country. King James the First of Scotland was very upset with the ruckus the ball game caused and went even further, declaring in 1424 that *"Na man play at the Fute-ball"*. Perhaps his team kept losing.

So by medieval times Britain was already in the grip of football fever.

Moving along another half century and dribbling and areas marked out for the game had come into existence as the manuscript collection of the miracles of King Henry VI of England testifies:

". . . is called by some the foot-ball game. It is one in which young men, in country sport, propel a huge ball not by throwing it into the air but by striking it and rolling it along the ground and that not with their hands but with their feet . . ".

King Henry VIII reputedly bought the first pair of football boots in 1526, and football had become much more organised by then. By 1581 English schools were providing reports of *"parties" or "sides", "judges over the parties" and "training masters". But although the violence had lessened it still raised its head. In 1595 a document stated: "Gunter's son and ye Gregorys fell together . . . at football. Old Gunter drew his dagger and both broke their heads, and they died both within a fortnight after".*

By the 1600s, football was an established and increasingly popular part of British life and references to it had found their way into the literature of the day. In 1608, Shakespeare had King Lear say, *"Nor tripped neither, you base football player". This was the first time "football" had been spelt in the modern manner. " . . . lusty shepherds try their force at football, care of victory . . . They ply their feet, and still the restless ball, toss'd to and fro, is urged by them all".* That was the English Poet Edmund Waller (c.1624). *"The streete (in London) being full of footballs".* That was the famous diarist Samuel Pepys in 1665.

In Manchester in 1608 the local authorities complained that: *"With the ffotebale . . . there hath beene greate disorder in our towne of Manchester we are told, and glasse windowes broken . . . by a companie of lewd and disordered persons using that unlawful exercise of playing with the ffotebale in ye streets of the said towne . . ".*

Must have been visiting fans ...

Football had come so far by 1660 that a book was written about it, the first objective study of the game in England. The author was Francis Willoughby and he called his work the Book of Sports. It refers to goals and pitches, (goalkeeping had already been established by this time) to scoring and selecting teams and striking balls through goals. There is also a basic sketch of a football pitch and mention that a rule had been introduced so that players could not strike their opponent higher than the ball otherwise they often *". . . break one another's shins when two meet and strike together against the ball".*

Even though football was often outlawed in many areas of the country, with violators threatened with imprisonment, it remained popular even amongst aristocrats. *"Lord Willoughby . . . with so many of their servants . . . play'd a match at foot-ball against such a number of Countrymen, where my Lord of Sunderland being busy about the ball, got a bruise in the breast".*

Football was really put on the map in 1681 when King Charles II of England attended a game between the Royal Household and George Monck, 1st Duke of Albemarle's servants. Football was here to stay.

In the 1800s, when the working man's day lasted twelve hours or more and six days a week, the only men who had enough leisure to indulge in football were the wealthy. Their sons at private schools were encouraged to play to develop a competitive spirit and keep themselves fit and so the rules developed that produced the game as we know it today. Nonetheless, there were a variety of rules regulating the matches so in 1848 Mr. H. de Winton and Mr. J. C. Thring called a meeting at Cambridge University with twelve representatives from other schools; their eight-hour discussions produced the first set of modern rules, the Cambridge rules.

So in the truth, mankind has probably been throwing and kicking anything from monkey heads to coconuts and turnips since before he could walk upright. But there are at least 3,000 years of history behind the football match of today.

The millennia have passed and football, soccer, has become one of the most exciting mass entertainments of all time.

THE FOOTBALL LEAGUE

Clubs dedicated solely to the sport of football were formed regularly throughout the 18th century. The London Gymnastic Society was one of the first created in the 1850s. The first club to be referred to as a club was the *"Foot-Ball Club of Edinburgh"* in Scotland in the period 1821 to 1824. Great Leicestershire Cricket and Football Club existed in 1840. The staff of Guy's Hospital in London formed Guys Hospital Football Club in 1843 which claims to be the oldest known football club, whilst Sheffield Football Club founded in 1857, is the oldest club documented as not being affiliated to a school, university or other institution. The oldest club still playing association football is Cambridge University Association Football Club.

Soon, club names that are recognisable to fans today were appearing; Bolton Wanderers (1874), Aston Villa (1874), Queen's Park (1867), Sheffield Wednesday (1867); and of course there was a certain Newton Heath LYR Football Club which was formed by railway workers in 1878. What would they say today about the extraordinary club they started?

The time had come to try and make a set of rules that would be adhered to by all the clubs. In 1862, thirteen London clubs met and hammered out regulations to govern the sport. This led to the formation of the Football Association in 1863 to oversee regulations for the sport.

No history of football would be complete if the name of Ebenezer Cobb Morely was not mentioned. He was a central figure in bringing the Football Association into being. He was a player himself and a founding member of the Football Association. As captain of his team, the Barnes Club, he proposed a governing body for the sport and so the meeting of the thirteen London clubs came about. From 1863-1866 he was the FA's first secretary and from 1867-1874 its second president. He drafted the *"London Rules"* at his home in Barnes in London.

Another event must be mentioned here: the first official, international game between England and Scotland took place in November 1872 on the West of Scotland cricket ground in Partick, Scotland. 4,000 spectators watched a 0-0 draw although the Scots had a goal disallowed. The very first game had taken place on the 5th March 1870 at the Oval cricket ground in London.

Most of the men playing in the teams at the time were amateurs, although betting had long been a feature of the sport. On the 18th July 1885 it was finally decided that football could become a professional sport. But clubs were still setting their own fixture dates and the whole structure was chaotic. Now was the moment for another man to step into the limelight, Mr. William McGregor, a director of Aston villa Football Club and to make his mark on history.

It was the 2nd March 1888. McGregor wrote to the committees of several football clubs to propose that a league competition would guarantee a certain number of fixtures and bring some order into the

Original Handwritten Rules 1863

confusion that then existed. In Anderson's Hotel in London on the 23rd March 1888, on the eve of the FA Cup Final, a meeting was held to discuss the proposal. Manchester was once again in the headlines when on the 17th April at the Royal Hotel, a final meeting created the Football League.

On the 8th September 1888, twelve clubs Accrington, Aston Villa, Blackburn Rovers, Derby County, Everton, Notts County, Preston North End, Stoke, FC., West Bromwich Albion and Wolverhampton Wanderers, sent their players out onto the turf for the first games in the new football league season.

Only once the season was underway was it decided that clubs would play against one another twice, once at home and once away, with two points awarded for a win and one for a draw. For the record, Preston won the first league title without losing a single game and won the FA Cup Final, too, the first league-FA Cup double.

Three clubs dominated during those first exciting years; Preston North End, Aston Villa and Sunderland; for fourteen seasons only three other clubs would win league titles; Everton, Sheffield United and Liverpool.

In 1892 the league expanded with the addition of a new Second Division. Liverpool, Arsenal and Newcastle United were now on the scene and a new name had been added to the First Division. A club with a glorious future had made its first steps to the top. Fourteen years had passed since they had first formed but now Newton Heath had arrived in the First Division.

Six years later, 1898, the number of clubs in each league had increased to eighteen and automatic promotion and relegation for two clubs was introduced the same year.

The Third Division was only added after WWI in 1921. By then another host of names that would later become legendary, including Tottenham Hotspur, Chelsea and Fulham, had been added to divisions that by 1905 had been boosted in numbers to 20 clubs in each. There were two third divisions in fact, the Third Division North and the Third Division South. Newton Heath by that time had become Manchester United having changed their name and moved to Old Trafford in 1902.

With the coming of WWII, the league was suspended for seven seasons. In 1950 there were 24 clubs in each of the two third divisions so there were now 92 league clubs. The third division clubs were amalgamated into a single division abolishing regionalisation and the Fourth Division was added in 1958. Four clubs could be promoted and relegated in the lower two divisions. In divisions one and two until 1974, two clubs made the climb or fell; the number was increased to three that same year.

The league now entered a period of calm with only minor changes such as altering the points system, three instead of two for a win introduced in 1981, and goal differences being taken into account. There was one enormous change ahead, however.

On May 27th 1992 the Premier League was formed. All First Division clubs resigned together from the Football League, which now operated with three divisions. The old system of interaction between the leagues, however, did not change but 104 years of tradition were over. The elite clubs were now, literally, in a league of their own. Money had tempted the top clubs and lucrative television rights deals beckoned them. The deal will soon be worth three billion pounds.

This wealth, of course, makes it almost impossible for a promoted club to compete with the big boys in the first season after promotion, and relegation often follows immediately. But the rewards for the successful are enormous with British Premier League clubs amongst the richest in the world and able to buy in players to make the....

....terraces on a Saturday afternoon one of the most thrilling places to be.

William McGregor regarded as the founder of the Football League

IN THE BEGINNING

The Chelsea story begins with the ambition of two men; Henry Augustus 'Gus' Mears, and his brother Joseph T. Mears. Augustus Mears was an English businessman with an interest in football, who was born in 1873, and by 1896 the brothers were searching for a suitable stadium in which to stage top-rank football matches. When the owner of an arena at Stamford Bridge died, the brothers, who had both played football, seized their opportunity, and the legend began.

The Stamford Bridge stadium had been officially opened on the 28th of April 1877 and was first used by the London Athletic Club. It belonged to former athletes, the Waddell brothers, wealthy financiers, and was intended to provide a prestigious venue for sporting events. The name of the ground is derived from a stream called Stanford Creek, which ran along behind what is now the east stand, and two bridges that crossed the stream. One of these originally bore the name, Sanford Bridge; this was later changed to Little Chelsea Bridge. From these three names emerged Stamford Bridge. Incidentally, the ground is situated in the London Borough of Hammersmith and Fulham, not Chelsea. Then the ground passed into the hands of John Stunt, in 1883. He died in 1902, and negotiations began with the Mears brothers that year, with the stadium finally becoming theirs on the 29th September 1904.

The story almost ended before it had begun, however, because Mears was unable to persuade Fulham FC Chairman Henry Norris to use the ground for his club's matches; Mears wanted £1,500 a year ground rent. Mears thought it might be better to sell the ground to the Great Western Railway company rather than try to find another football club to move in. Stamford Bridge almost became a coal yard.

The story behind the story: Stamford Bridge was saved by a dog. Mear's friend, Fred Parker, wanted Mears to go ahead with his original football club idea. Parker was passionate about football and calculated that the ground could yield £3,000 from each major event staged there. Parker met Mears, who told his friend that he could find no investors to put money into the new venture and wanted to sell the ground. When

Mear's dog bit Fred, "… so as to draw blood freely", as Parker said later, adding, " Scotch terrier; always bites before he speaks", Mears was impressed with the man's reaction, commenting, "You took that bite well … get that bite seen to, and meet me here at nine tomorrow morning and we'll get busy".

Whether the story is true or not, Mears decided to keep the ground and form his own football team. At a meeting held in the Rising Sun pub opposite Stamford Bridge on the 14th of March, 1905, a name for the club was decided upon. Kensington FC.

Well, it might have been. Or perhaps, London and Stamford Bridge FC., because both names were considered.

Mears placed an announcement in 'The Times' newspaper: 'It has been decided to form a professional football club, called the Chelsea Football Club, for Stamford Bridge".

Archibald Leitch, the foremost designer of grandstands of his time, was hired and submitted his plans to alter the stadium, on the 23rd of February 1905; 100,000 fans would soon be able to watch the games. Leitch would go on to design major stadiums such as Ibrox, Twickenham, Anfield and Highbury.

Understandably, Chelsea wanted to gain admission to the Southern League, but following objections by Fulham and Tottenham Hotspur they were denied entry. That's neighbours for you. Mears decided to apply to the Football League.

The Football League met in May to consider whether or not to accept the new club in its ranks. After much lobbying behind the scenes and an inspirational speech on the day by former London Athletic official Fred Parker, (of dog bite fame) representing the club, the vote went Chelsea's way. It was the 29th of May 1905. The club was in the league and the blue surge was underway. Hull City, Leeds City and Clapton Orient also joined the league that year, and the team adopted the Chelsea Pensioner image for their club badge, although the players never wore it on their shirts. It was to remain associated with the club until 1952 and was the reason the team were known as, **'The Pensioners'.**

9

Chelsea Team 1905

THE EARLY YEARS

Chelsea began their road to football greatness in League Division Two, and despite losing their first match to Stockport , 1-0, they showed that they meant business from the start. The club's first manager was also a player, a half-back. John Robertson was a Scottish international, and he scored the only goal in Chelsea's 1-0 victory over Blackpool in the Pensioners' second match, their first victory and their first league win of the season.

Revenge is sweet, and Chelsea walloped Stockport 6-0 at home in 1906. It was one of a string of impressive goal tallies that proved that Robertson's men were destined for greater things. Chelsea also thrashed Barnsley 6-0, Lincoln 7-0, Port Vale 7-0, Orient 6-0 and Leeds 4-0.

The club was soon recruiting established players from other teams, and so England international William *"Fatty" Foulke, a 6'3"*, 22-stone goalkeeper, made his way to Stamford Bridge from Sheffield United, as did inside- forward James Edwin 'Jimmy' Windridge. Foulkes saved a penalty in the first match against Stockport County, even though new rules forced him to stay static on the goal line.

At the end of that first season, with 38 games played, Chelsea finished in a very respectable third place. They had lost just 7 matches, and the club would have to wait until the 1983/84 season before fans could celebrate losing less than that. (For the record, they lost 4 that season.)

Unfortunately, a poor run at the end of the season, when they did not win any of their last five games, put paid to their promotion hopes. With 53 points, they were 13 points adrift of leaders Bristol City. 12 points behind Manchester United, with whom they had drawn both league matches. Frank Pearson was top goalscorer with 18 goals. Willie Foulke in goal saved all 10 penalties he faced, and only Ross Turnbull could equal that 100% record by saving all 4 penalties that he faced between 2009 and 2012.

Full of optimism the club entered the 1906/1907 season. Although they just missed the top spot, they finished in second place only three points behind Nottingham Forest and secured promotion to the First Division in only their second season in the league. It was a magnificent start for the club. The team was attracting large crowds, and on Good Friday 1906, a crowd of 67,000 attended the league game against Manchester United, which was a record for a London football match.

1907 was also the year that David Calderhead joined the club as secretary-manager and stayed for almost 26 years.

The club struggled in Division One. They could only manage 13th place at the end of the season following promotion, 1907/08. The subsequent season was little better; 11th. And then it got worse. 19th position in 1909/10. They were relegated to Division Two. It was a bitter pill for Mears to swallow.

Mears didn't know it or he might have despaired, but a pattern had developed which saw Chelsea riding up and down between the First and Second Divisions for remainder of the pre-First World War years.

In 1911/12 they came second to Derby County with an equal number of points, 54, went back up to the First Division and only narrowly escaped an immediate descent by scraping home in 18th place.

Just before the Great War struck,

Chelsea were beginning to find their form again and were 8th when the 1913/14 season ended.

"Football will be played as far as possible", was the message from the Chelsea board of directors when war was declared. No one expected the fracas in France to last

long, and the lads would be back to watch or play the game again in the new year, wouldn't they?

When they weren't and tens of thousands more were sent to the front lines in the new year instead, there were calls for football to be suspended for the duration of the fighting.

The matches continued, and a percentage of the takings from the games was donated to the Prince of Wales' war fund, but the atmosphere everywhere was one of gloom. Chelsea donated 50 footballs to the lads at the front, but the time was fast approaching when more would be required.

A 'Footballers' Battalion, the 17th Service Battalion of the Middlesex Regiment, the 'Die-Hards', had been formed by William Joynson-Hick, MP for Brentford, in December 1914. Two of Chelsea's star players, Viv Woodward and local man Harry Ford, were among the first Chelsea men to join up. They were volunteers; conscription did not begin until 1916.

By the end of the season in 1915, club gate receipts were down by fifty percent. All players had been put on amateur status by the FA. Chelsea played in the FA Cup final — known as the 'Khaki' Cup final because there were so many men in uniform watching — at Old Trafford, but lost to Sheffield United, 3-0. As they finished in 19th place in the league once more, they would certainly have been relegated if pressure from the War Office and the public had not put an end to professional football for the remainder of the war.

Almost half of the Chelsea staff picked up uniforms and rifles, and many of them, of course, never returned from the battlefields of France, and the Somme especially. Nine Bradford City players lost their lives. The 17th and 23rd Middlesex sent over 8,000 officers and men into some of the hardest battles of the war. The soldiers were former players from many of the clubs including Chelsea, West Ham, Clapton Orient and Liverpool. Donald Bell, a defender with Bradford City, and Bernard Vann, a centre-forward at Derby County, both won the Victoria cross for exceptional bravery. Neither survived the war. Chelsea's Vivian Woodward was badly injured in the thigh by a German hand grenade. He was sent back to England, and although

he returned to the front in August 1916, he managed to survive the war.

The clubs engaged in regional league competitions and friendlies for the remainder of the war years. Chelsea's chairman, William Claude Kirby, was a major force in helping to establish a London Combination tournament. This consisted of 12 teams. Chelsea won

11

Alex Raisbeck 1896

the tournament in early 1916. They also Won the War Fund Cup in 1918 against West Ham.

In 1919 the league clubs opened their gates for professional league football once more. The minimum wage was now £10 per week, but later it was reduced to £8.00; £6.00 during the closed season. A Chelsea side had won the Victory Cup that year, beating Fulham 3-0.

Fortunately for Chelsea, the League had decided to expand the number of clubs in the First Division by two clubs, so Arsenal came up from Division Two, and Chelsea remained in the top drawer.

It was time for a Chelsea star, Bob Whittingham, a prolific goalscorer, to move on, having scored 80 goals in 129 appearances for the Pensioners. His talent and 26 goals had played a considerable role in getting Chelsea back in to the First Division in 1911/12. He had also scored a penalty in the thrilling first match of the season against title-holders Everton, helping the Pensioners to a 3-2 victory.

In his stead, along came a future Chelsea and England favourite, centre-forward John Gilbert 'Jack' Cock from Huddersfield, for a record fee of £2,500. Cock struck gold in his first season with Chelsea, hitting home 21 goals in the league and 254 in all competitions. Although he could not maintain his form in the subsequent two seasons, he was still top goalscorer at the club. To quote one newspaper report, he gave, *"The best centre forward exhibition ever"*, when England played Scotland.

There were six players in the team who had played with Chelsea before the war; Harold Halse, Walter Bettridge, Laurence Abrams, Jack Harrow and goalkeeper James Molyneux. Molyneux was now in his late 30s and his place in the team was being challenged by war hero Colin Hampton. Hampton had received the Military Medal for Gallantry in Mesopotamia.

Chelsea started off fiercely with two wins from two games, only to flounder and lose four of the next five games. The Blues then recovered their momentum, only to lose three of their last 5 games to finish third in the league table, having reached the FA Cup

semi-finals, where they lost 3-1 to Aston Villa. Nonetheless, the hope was that this time, perhaps, the run of inconsistency could be broken. The club, which had always attracted the artistic and trendy Londoners to its games, could also count the Kings of Britain and Spain amongst the spectators. Stamford Bridge had hosted the Cup Final in 1920, which brought in £13,414 from the 72,805 spectators. The club bought international players, who added glamour to the game. There was good reason to look forward with hope.

Except that the team was aging. Calderhead delegated coaching to the trainer and was rather impersonal in his relationships with players. This attitude was reflected in the performances. Players made individual efforts, but the team lacked cohesiveness. Chelsea were soon up to their old tricks and were in 18th place at the season's end.

There was an enormous distraction for all involved in the club that season.

In 1921, the club was embroiled in a corruption affair uncovered by an FA enquiry. The stadium improvements in 1920/21 were found to have been carried out without a tendering process or any plans being submitted for assessment. The contractor turned out to be J. T. Mears' own company, which he had given a profit margin of 20 percent. The overly-long period of work was supervised by one of Mears' employees and was faulty, entailing a continuous series of repairs. Mears had also tried to bind the club to a catering contract and overcharge them for buying the Stamford Bridge ground.

Chelsea were in 9th position at the end of the following season and seemed to have put the turmoil over J. T Mears behind them.

But in 1923 they were back down to 19th, so there were nervous fans as the 1923/24 season got under way. The anxiety proved to be warranted.

Chelsea went down in their first two games, first 3-0 against Blackburn Rovers and then at home 0-1 to Tottenham Hotspur.

September started well, with revenge wins against Blackburn and

Tottenham and hope was reborn; until the end of the month. Defeat against Sheffield United heralded a run of 13 games that yielded just one victory. It was indicative that Scottish international Andrew Wilson, one of the best centre-forwards of his generation, who joined Chelsea at the end of the year, was top scorer that season but could only net 5 league goals. It was one of the worst tallies for a top goalscorer ever recorded at Chelsea. 6 defeats in 11 matches in 1924 put paid to any hopes Chelsea supporters still had of remaining in the First Division. Despite winning the last 4 matches, including

two impressive victories, 4-1 against Sunderland and 3-1 against Manchester United, Chelsea hit 21st position. After losing a play-off over two legs against Middlesbrough, they were relegated. A bitter blow for a club that boasted such talented players as John Cock, Jack Harrow (who spent his entire career at Chelsea), and Thomas Meehan, one of the best half-backs in England.

So Chelsea joined their later great rivals Manchester United, who had already been demoted, in the Second Division for the 1924/25 season. They would not see the First Division again until 1930. And

His Majesty The King talks to some of the players 21st February 1920

1929 Chelsea Team

when Manchester climbed back into Division One in 1925, Chelsea were left adrift of the leaders in Division Two, in 5th place. They had started well with only two losses in 23 games before they lost power again, losing all but two of the last six matches. Andy Wilson had netted 10 goals, but it was William Whitton who was top goalscorer with 16.

The club started on its second season in the Second Division desperately hoping to do better. They did, but it was still not good enough to get back to the top division.

1925 was the year that the offside rule in English football was changed. Now, only two players needed to be between the attacker and the goal line when the ball was last played, not three.

"It was hoped that the alteration … would make for improvement, but unhappily expectations have not been realised", moaned 'The Times' newspaper one year later. 'The Daily Mirror', however, called the change *"revolutionary"*. The number of offside offences was dramatically reduced, and the number of goals scored in the league rose equally dramatically from 4,700 the previous season, to 6,373.

Chelsea put the new tactics to good use and exploited the new attacking possibilities the rule opened up. They tightened their defence, too, and only Derby County and Sheffield Wednesday had conceded less goals at the end of the season than Chelsea's 49. But once again, despite a 14-match undefeated run at the beginning of the season, a slump in December and January and again in April meant a third place after the final whistle of the season. Bob Turnbull had joined the team in 1925 and rediscovered his form by becoming top goalscorer with 29 goals. He repeated his form the following year as top goalscorer with 17 goals, scoring 58 from 87 appearances with the Blues in three seasons. And although the purse strings were tight that year, a future legend arrived in the summer; Simeon 'Sam' Millington would become the new goalkeeping hero at Stamford Bridge.

The Pensioners fared no better in their third season in the Second Division. Between two losses on the 11th of December 1926 and the 9th of March 1927 when Chelsea lost to Cardiff in the 6th round of the FA Cup, lay a run that produced nine wins and just three games drawn. Thereafter they wilted and could not win one of the last five games, so they rolled in fourth, 10 points behind the leaders, Middlesbrough who had 62 points.

This was the season when Benjamin Howard Baker was replaced between the goalposts by Sam Millington, and full-back Tommy Law came to the club, becoming a popular and long-serving member, whose slide tackles were legendary; Law stayed until 1939. The team were not helped by Turnbull being handed out a two-month suspension by the FA for an incident in October 1926.

There was no more comfort to be had in 1927/28. 8 wins had brought joy to the hearts of Chelsea supporters at the end of the year 1927. Just 5 points lost them the leadership, and the loss of 4 out of the last five matches did the damage, so Jimmy Thompson's 25 goals could not lift the curse. Neither could the 6 matches in which the Pensioners scored 4 or more goals.

Thompson made an immeasurable contribution to the club when he returned after WWII as chief scout. Persuasive and personable, he was one of Chelsea's great characters; he was responsible for many famous players signing for the team, such as Jimmy Greaves and Terry Venables. Thompson died in 1984.

Chelsea fought their way through another season that brought them no rewards and only 9th place. It was beginning to look as though the Second Division was going to be their permanent home. As usual their form was erratic. The started off like rockets, winning seven of the first eight games. Yet at the end they had fizzled out, to win just two of the last eleven matches, which meant that they had won just 17 of the 42 games that season. The FA Cup seemed as elusive as ever, and they only got as far as the 5th round when they lost against Portsmouth away from home.

Over the summer, David Calderhead agreed to his players taking part in a series of matches in South America against representative teams such as Brazilian side Sao Paolo, Boca Juniors, Racing Club of Argentina and the Olympic champions of Uruguay. The Pensioners played beneath floodlights for the first time — these were unknown in London — and had numbers on their shirts; another first. This led to them being called, 'Los Numerados' (the numbered ones). They were the first club, alongside Arsenal, to wear numbered shirts, ten years before the Football League introduced the practice in the league.

Over the three-month tour, some of the stadia they played in were huge; 100,000 spectators crowded into the Centenario Stadium in the Uruguayan capital, Montevideo. They won several games and lost others, going down against Racing Club 0-4, 3-4 against Boca Juniors and drawing with Sao Paola in the first of two games, 4-4. They beat a Buenos Aires team 3-2 and won their second match against Montevideo 2-1. Calderhead's men could be proud of themselves, for the Montevideo side was almost entirely made up of players who were in the national team.

It was an incredible experience for the Chelsea men, and when they returned home for the new season, it seemed as though there was a new team spirit on the field. They still lost 4 of the first 9 games, but won the other five so it was difficult to tell what might happen later. The next 9 games produced only one defeat.

Along came Chelsea's major signing that year, although it may not have seemed so at the time. George 'The Bomb' Mills was an amateur player, a huge centre-forward who had been singularly unimpressive before his arrival at Stamford Bridge. His debut for Calderhead's men came on December the 21st against Preston North End when he scored in a 5-0 rout of the northerners. A new star was born, and Mills would stay with Chelsea until the end of his career. He became a prolific goalscorer, notching up 14 goals in the 20 games remaining that season and going on to net 125 in 239 games.

Hope had returned to Stamford Bridge, and the players did not let it leave again. George Pearson and Harry Miller were also getting through to the goal. As May approached, the battle for second place was intense. Rivals Oldham were two points behind Chelsea, but their goal average was better. If they won their final match and Calderhead's men lost, Oldham would be promoted. Nervous, the Blues blew it at Bury losing 1-0, but Oldham went down to Barnsley 2-1. The Pensioners had lost 3 of their last 8 games, but fortunately they had won 5 of them, and their 55 points were enough for 2nd place behind Blackpool on 58. 25 years after their formation, Chelsea were back in Division One with the big boys.

The new season brought more joy for the Chelsea supporters. Hughie Gallacher joined the team from Newcastle for a massive £10,000. He joined alongside two more new singings, Scottish forwards Alex Jackson and Alec Cheyne.

Gallacher soon joined the list of Chelsea legends. At 5' 5", the Scottish international was small, but compensated for his lack of height with an astoundingly powerful jump. He was also a prolific goalscorer using either foot to thump the ball towards the goal or skillfully dribble around three or four players at once. He scored five goals in a game on four occasions.

Sadly his talent was paired with indiscipline, and his private life was fraught. He often swore at officials and players, and on one occasion he was banned for two-months for swearing at a referee. His drinking habits led to him being thrown out of a pub on the King's Road in Chelsea. He was always ready for the match, however, and became Chelsea's top scorer during his four seasons with the team, scoring 81 goals in total. He was so popular that when he went

with Chelsea to Newcastle for a match against his old team, 68,386 people turned out to watch the game, a record attendance at St. James' Park.

There were mighty wins and mighty defeats in this first year back in Division One. The Pensioners beat Manchester United 6-2 and then lost 6-2 to Derby County; they thrashed Sunderland 5-0 and crashed 5-1 to Arsenal.

They lost their drive again at the end of the season as so often but hit a respectable 12th place after the last game. They had reached the quarter-finals of the FA Cup, too, although they lost to Birmingham 3-0 in the replay. It seemed right to be optimistic.

By the time the 1930/31 season had got under way, Sam Millington was gradually relinquishing his place between the posts to the young Vic Woodley. Woodley was a first-class keeper, who would play more than 252 League matches for the Blues. He liked to leave his line to get to crosses, which was a brave action, because the tactic was not usual in those days.

The Stamford Bridge ground had remained largely unchanged since it had been built. In 1930 a huge bank of terracing was erected at the Shed End, which from then on, was to become home for die-hard Chelsea supporters.

Calderhead had talented players but not the ability to make form them into a consistently cohesive unit, it seemed. This was proved by a run of thirteen matches at the start of the season in which the team only won three. At that rate, life at the top was likely to be short-lived. Chelsea managed to rally in December and started a run of seventeen games with just two losses, finishing the season in 12th position. Gate receipts were boosted by a record crowd of 75,334 against Arsenal, and the FA Cup had brought an exciting run up to the semi-finals, even though it ended in defeat to Newcastle, 2-1.

True to form, on the back of a season of excitement, 1932/33 brought disappointment. Chelsea struggled to make headway from the start, losing three games in a row on three separate occasions and receiving a drubbing by Leeds United, 6-0. They were lucky to

Huge crowds for third round English Cup tie against Luton Town at the Stamford Bridge 12th January 1935

escape with their heads above water on 18th place, just 2 points clear of the relegation zone clubs. It was time for David Calderhead to bow to the inevitable and he finally handed over power, to Leslie Knighton as secretary manager. The change did nothing to stop the rot, and the following season they were even worse off, in 19th position. Team injuries had been a continuous problem for the new manager throughout 1933/34.

In November 1934, the legend that was Hughie Gallacher had become an unreliable team player, and his days at Stamford Bridge came to an end. His drinking and nights out had taken their toll on his performances, so Gallacher was sold to Derby County for £2,750. Winger Dickie Spence from Barnsley, and Linfield and Ireland centre-forward Joe Bambrick came to strengthen the Chelsea ranks. Spence was to become an England international regular and set a Chelsea record for goals by a winger, netting 19 in his first season to become top goalscorer, beating Bambrick's 15. Bambrick's reputation led to the coining of the phrase, *"Head, heel or toe, slip it to Joe"*.

Spence would go on to become a major figure off the field at Stamford Bridge, when he used his knowledge to train the likes of Bonetti, Brabrook, Bridges, Greaves, Harris, Hollins, Houseman, Hudson, Murray, Osgood, Sillett, Tambling, Tindall and Venables.

The team were able to better the previous season's lacklustre performance, finishing in May in 12th position.

They did even better in 1935/36, getting themselves up to 8th in the league table with exciting, attacking football that saw goal numbers by Mills, Spence, Bambrick and Burgess all get to double figures. But the team crashed out of the FA Cup in the 5th round, going down 3-2 in the replay against Fulham. Bambrick slotted home 19 goals to become the Pensioner's top goalscorer. Although their performances were still not on a par with the top teams, Chelsea could attract large crowds, and 82,905 filled the Stamford stadium for a match against Arsenal. It is still the largest official attendance record for the club. It remains the third largest attendance in the UK.

Meanwhile, off the field there was sadder news. The club's co-founder, Joseph Mears, passed away, as did long-serving Bert Palmer,

and Claude Kirby, the club's first chairman. Stamford Bridge was put into a trust which benefited Mears' three children, and Joe Mear Jnr. began to guide Chelsea's fate and did so for the next thirty years.

On a trip to Europe over the summer taking in Germany, it was impossible for the team to miss the amount of building projects that were taking place under the Nazi regime. But no one was worried. England was peaceful and football was foremost on the players' minds.

Chelsea players could sparkle, send a host of international players onto the pitch and attract crowds of well over 30,000 every week, yet no one seemed able to make the individual talents into a force to be reckoned with.

Winning 5 of the first 16 games in the 1936/37 season was not exactly the stuff of champions. George Mills made up for Bambrick's meagre 2 goals and just 10 appearances by hitting home 23, but it was another uneven season that brought a 3-0 defeat to Millwall in just the 4th round of the FA Cup. There was not a lot to cheer about with 13th place and 41 points; 16 points separated them from the league winners, Manchester City, but only 11 points separated them from last-placed Sheffield Wednesday.

With a 6-1 thrashing of Liverpool to start the 1937/38 season, fans could have been forgiven for hoping the tide had turned. But losing the next two away games proved that it hadn't. It was not a bad start with 8 wins from 14 matches, but there was the usual drought to contend with; 9 games without a win from the middle of December 1937 through to the middle of February 1938. The Pensioners had even topped the table for a brief, heady moment. Favourite Bambrick made just 3 appearances due to injury, and it was left to Mills to bang home 13 with outside-left Will Chitty scoring 11. Joe Payne had been brought in from Luton Town, scoring 4 goals in his ten matches of the season. It was not enough. Injuries and lack of form were holding the team back. And there was not much sign that anything was going to lift them away far from the 10th position that year, either. Bringing in the aging Ned Barkas to prop up the leaky defence was not designed to do the trick.

But the world was soon going to change dramatically. On the 14th of May 1938, captain Eddie Hapgood led an England side out

Division One.

Docherty had proven his credentials, proven that he could spot and encourage talent and motivate his players. He left an indelible memory of his tenure by replacing the white shorts with the blue that Chelsea still wear today.

Perhaps his young players were not quite up to speed as the new season began, because Chelsea only won 2 of their first 13 games and landed on 17th place. But then they hit their stride and began the long climb up the table, with Tambling and Bridges hitting the

net 19 and 15 times respectively. The FA Cup run was disappointing, with Chelsea going out to Huddersfield Town 2-1 at home in the 4th round, but there was a thrilling flourish at the end of the season with 7 wins from 9 games. Chelsea had fought their way to 5th place by the end of the season. They had drawn their games against Manchester United who were in 2nd place. They were back with a vengeance. The much-buffeted supporters could see great things coming their way.

Docherty had a magical squad lined up for the 1964/65 attempt

Chelsea v Tottenham Hotspur Jimmy Greaves takes flight to head the ball 31st March 1961

at glory. Bonetti, Bridges, Bert Murray, Tambling, Eddie McCreadie, Venables, Osgood, and George Graham, who had joined from Aston Villa.

The Blues made a terrific start. The football was based on high energy with quick passing. And there were innovative tactics — Docherty was one of the first managers to employ overlapping full-backs. 17 games with only one defeat, at home to Manchester United, 2-0, showed that they were a team to be reckoned with. They were on top of the table for much of the season and never lower than 3rd in the table, beating eventual runners-up Leeds United 2-0 in September. All looked rosy until March 1965 when a great FA Cup run came to an end in Chelsea's first semi-final for 13 years, against Liverpool. Chelsea lost 2-0. The dreaded wobbles began, and the

terrible last three games put paid to their league title hopes. In an incident that led to players being sent home after flouting a pre-match curfew set by Docherty, an under-strength team was clouted 6-2 by Burnley, and the club had to contend with 3rd place after losing the final match 3-2 to Blackpool. After the Burnley incident, Docherty's relationship with Bridges, Graham, and other players deteriorated, and this break down would soon lead to several players leaving the club. It was, as a journalist with 'The Times' wrote, *"A sad ending to their eight months of ceaseless challenge in league and cup"*. But the Blues had won the League Cup, thanks to a 3-2 away win in the first leg against Leicester City and 0-0 draw in the second. They had made it through to the semi-finals of the FA Cup where they lost to Liverpool 2-0, and for the first time, three players

Chelsea v Burnley Tussle between Morgan of Burnley and Venables, the Chelsea captain 21st August 1965

went over the 20-goal mark; Barry Bridges had a sensational season with 27 goals, making him top goalscorer; Bobby Tambling was also scintillating and only two behind Bridges with 25; George Graham hit 21 in his first season, and Bert Murray struck 18 times.

1965/66 was less successful on and off the pitch. Docherty may have been quick-witted and fun to be around, but the conflict between the volatile, temperamental manager and some of his players intensified. George Graham left the club. Bridges' talents were lost to Chelsea when he left as well, sold to Birmingham City of the Second Division for £55,000, a club record, in May 1966. His impressive scoring skills did not diminish at Birmingham. Terry

Venables was another player who departed the club in 1966.

The results for the season were mixed as Docherty tried to build a side that could win trophies, but which contained players that harboured resentment towards their manager. Nonetheless, in 12 games there were only two losses in all competitions, although five games were drawn. At the end of December 1965, the team began an encouraging run of 12 games with just one defeat, which gave fans hope that they had at last got into their stride. The Blues began to climb the table to 4th spot. Bobby Tambling and George Graham were hitting the target, 23 times each by the end of the season. But April brought 5 defeats, 3 in the league, one in the Fairs Cup and

The Docherty squad

1967 FA Cup Final Chelsea v Tottenham Hotspur Managers lead out the teams prior to the match 20th May 1967

also the FA Cup, and the season finished with a league game lost to Aston Villa, 2-0 and a drubbing by Barcelona, 5-0 in the Fairs Cup semi-final replay. It was 5th place for Chelsea that year in the league. Docherty knew he had to rethink.

Charlie Cooke was the man who replaced Venables. As broadcaster and author Rick Glanvill described it, Docherty had exchanged " … *an artisan for an artist*".

Docherty seemed to have found players that worked well together in 1996/97, and by the autumn there was new breath in the team, which was playing the kind of flowing football that excites the terraces. Chelsea were top of the table, unbeaten, and demolished both Aston Villa and Charlton Athletic 6-2. And then fate struck a cruel blow. In the game against Blackpool on October the 5th, Osgood was challenged by the Blackpool left-back Emlyn Hughes. Osgood went down with his right leg broken. The accident seemed to deflate the Blues and they managed just one league win in 10 games through November and December until January the 7th. Although Tambling was his usual goal-hungry self and scored 28, no one else got over the 20 mark. 2 wins from 6 at the end of the season 1967 did the rest of the~damage, and dropped Chelsea down to 9th at the season's end on 44 points. Leaders Manchester United were far away on 60.

There had been successes. Docherty's Diamonds reached the FA Cup final having dispensed with high-flying Leeds United along the way. They had also taken revenge on Sheffield Wednesday for clobbering them 6-1 in the league, by beating them 1-0 in the FA Cup quarter-final. The Blues could not quite make the wheel spin, however, and lost the final 2-1 to Tottenham.

Change was about come to Chelsea once more. And it was not for the better. Docherty had not just aggravated the players with his outbursts; the Chelsea board had come in for its share of abuse, and in October 1967…

…Docherty resigned, following allegations of racial abuse whilst on tour in Bermuda, and a one-month ban by the FA.

THE FA CUP AT LAST

Docherty had been moving away from a high-octane side to one with more subtlety by the time the 1967/68 season opened and when Docherty left, Ron Stuart took over for a few weeks before Dave Sexton arrived to take control of the Blues.

Sexton's managerial style was more subdued than Docherty's had been. He saw the weaknesses in what Docherty described as a team that was better than Manchester United in its potential. Sexton had started off as a coach at Chelsea before moving to Leyton Orient and Arsenal and then returning to Stamford Bridge.

He brought in Ian Hutchinson, David Webb and the truly ethereal Alan Hudson. 'Huddy', as he came to be known, was a strong and elegant midfielder, described as the 'closest thing Chelsea had to a Brazilian'.

At first, after a worrying few weeks at the start of the season when Chelsea rested between 19th and 16th positions following 16 games with just two wins, it seemed that Sexton was going to maintain the momentum that Docherty had built up. 'Huddy' made only one appearance, but with Peter Osgood working his tall magic as top goalscorer that season, hitting home 17 goals, Bobby Tambling still

Dave Sexton, signs autographs for young fans at Stamford Bridge 23rd October 1967

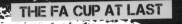

on form with 15 and forward Tommy Baldwin netting 17, the Blues were able to reach a respectable 6th place. The following year they had climbed up another place and were 5th, well placed to launch a title challenge the following season, or so it appeared to supporters.

It was an optimistic club that entered the 1969/70 season and that optimism proved to be justified and the fans were set cheering to the end. It was Osgood's year, too, as he walloped home a terrific 31 goals. Ian Hutchinson was no slouch either and hit the net 22 times. Midfield defender, Irishman John Dempsey even passed the opposition keepers three times as Chelsea rose to third place when the season was two-thirds of the way through. But the real excitement was taking place in the FA Cup playoffs.

The FA Cup run culminated in Chelsea reaching the final. Their opponents were Leeds United, the reigning league champions and the high flyers of the time, Chelsea's bitter adversaries. Leeds were

a hard, if not to say brutal side, yet despite the Blues' elegant play, Sexton's men knew how to look after themselves, too. It would prove to be a battle of the giants. The Wembley pitch was soggy and unworthy of hosting the final. Chelsea were coming off second best for most of the match. Blues supporters suffered agonies as their team fought back from behind, twice, first with a Houseman goal and then, after an excruciating wait, a late equaliser four minutes from full time was headed home by Hutchinson. A Wembley Cup Final had ended in a draw for the first time in its history.

Old Trafford witnessed a mammoth struggle in the replay. Fans were treated to a match of brute physical force and scintillating skill in what has been described as one of the best finals ever. Cooke's cross saw a diving header from Osgood hit the Leed's net to bring Chelsea back into the game after Leeds had gone ahead. The fans' nerves were stretched taught when extra time began. But a mighty

Peter Bonetti weighs up his options 15th March 1969

Chelsea lads celebrate the FA Cup win in 1970

throw from Ian Hutchinson met the head of the lurking Webb and when the final whistle blew, Chelsea had subdued the northerners 2-1 and emerged into the brilliant light of FA Cup glory.

Chelsea had gone through seven FA Cup semi-finals and three finals to lift the coveted trophy at last.

The FA Cup win opened the door for more excitement and hope of even more silverware, on the international scene, because Chelsea had now qualified for the UEFA Cup Winner's Cup.

They set off into Europe dispensing with Aris Thessaloniki and CSKA Sofia before meeting Club Brugge in the quarter-finals. Chelsea put the fans through the wringer again in this encounter. They lost the first leg 2-0 and few held any hope for progress in the replay. The tension and drama were high as the Blues battled to stay in the competition. They managed by a whisker. Only nine minutes from the end of normal time did the faithful Osgood relieve the strain and hit the second goal to force extra time. But when the match ended there was no doubt about the better team. Chelsea emerged 4-0 winners and would face Manchester City in the semi-final. City could not stop the blue flood, either, and Chelsea were in the final at the first attempt.

Now Chelsea would have to pull out all the stops because they were up against Real Madrid. But Sexton's men were not about to relinquish the dream without a fight, and in Greece, Osgood and Cooke again formed a lethal duo that pushed Chelsea ahead with seconds to go. A last desperate effort from Madrid got past the Chelsea keeper and the Spaniards had scraped a 1-1 draw. That was still the score at the end of extra time.

The replay took place just two days later.

It was defender Dempsey who put the Blues ahead with a magnificent goal, one of his rare scores, but the Irishman had never struck one that was as vital. The fans' hearts beat harder until Osgood wrote his name into the Chelsea history books with the goal that sank the Spaniards. The score was 2-1 to the London club at full-time, and Chelsea had won their first European honour. Sexton had given

Chelsea a wonderful season to cherish.

Unpredictability had followed Chelsea FC like a faithful hound throughout its helter-skelter journey to the top. Now it came licking their heels again. The possible reasons for this have provided food for generations of columnists' analytical powers. And presumably will do so for many more. Having hit the heights, Chelsea proceeded to plunge like a blue stone. The fall was barely perceptible at first. 6th place in 1970/71 and 7th in 1971/72 — when the squad singing 'Blue is the Colour', which became an anthem for the era, reached number five in the pop charts — did not seem to warn of a dramatic problem. There were two records that season, too; a 13-0 home win led to a 21-0 aggregate Cup Winner's Cup win over Jeunesse Hautcharage from Luxembourg, a record score line that remains unchallenged. Chelsea were knocked out later by Åtvidabergs FF.

Who?

And more importantly, why?

Nonetheless, Osgood was still enthralling to watch and another 31 goals were added to his tally that season. With Tommy Baldwin and John Hollins on 18 apiece there was not too much to worry about. Was there?

The FA Cup challenge petered out against Leyton Orient when Chelsea threw away a 2-goal lead. The League Cup went west when underdogs Stoke City beat Chelsea in the final. The Blues fell behind in that match but came back through an Osgood goal and then found their form again. But when Mulligan was injured and Sexton swopped Houseman to left back and brought on Baldwin, the gears stopped working and Eastman put in the winner for City.

Off the field, personal problems within the team were beginning to inflame. Sexton was entangled in arguments with Osgood, Baldwin and Hudson, concerning their lifestyles. At one point Hudson and Osgood were suspended. The dissent simmered and came to a head in 1973. Many players became involved and as Charlie Cooke said, " I think we were all a bit churlish, a bit immature about it ... the financial background was discomforting ... remember, the ground was getting rebuilt ... it was

Ron Harris Leads out Chelsea 1971

a pretty depressing time". Sexton was obstinate and the players' responses were unnecessarily juvenile and self-defeating.

During the 1972/73 season these antagonisms began to feed into the players' performances on the field.

On the 11th November 1972, Chelsea lost to Liverpool 3-1 and the rot set in. A slow dip at first and then they went into a more unsettling dive. One of the infamous series of 5 runs, 5 defeats tumbled the team in March 1973 as they struggled to finish on 12th place. Hutchinson had appeared just four times.

It was a fractured team, uneasy with itself that began the new season, 1973/74. Four lost games from the first five, two of those at home, proved to any doubters that here was a team in trouble. They hit the bottom of the table. The defeats began to pile up culminating in the loss of three of the last five matches. The other two resulted in draws. There followed a terrible defeat at home to West Ham on Boxing Day 1973. Chelsea had led 2—0 at half-time, but by full-time they had lost 2-4. Osgood and Hudson were put on the transfer list in January 1974. Less than one month later, Hudson had joined Stoke City. Sexton's concern seemed justified on one count; Hudson suffered from alcohol problems later in life. Dempsey and Webb

41

Peter Osgood 1969

(L-R) Tommy Baldwin, Steve Kember, Alan Hudson and Ron Harris form a defensive wall 1971

were also unhappy. Osgood 8 goals, Hutchinson 3 by the end of the season told its own sorry tale as the side limped home to 17th position. The board would have to make a hard decision soon.

Setting out in the 1974/75 season, the team initially gave the impression that they might survive the knife-wielding behind the scenes. The start was wobbly, but two losses from 8 games was hardly a disaster. Then, after 3 defeats in succession in September, the axe fell on Sexton, too. *"The object is to win the championship, and the board felt that we had no chance of doing this"*, was the comment from the chairman.

With the turmoil complete, the team could only notch up 8 wins from then until the end of the season. They settled on 21st place. The fall from grace was absolute, and the Blues had been relegated again.

Low gates, relegation, and financial difficulties were not guaranteed to tempt a top-class manager to replace Sexton. Chelsea legend Frank Blunstone turned down the job. Sexton's assistant Suart stepped into the breach for the next six months before former left-back Eddie McCready took control of the club's fate. His task was gargantuan.

The modern East Stand was being built and draining the club's finances. The plan was to create a 60,000 all-seater stadium described as *"The most ambitious ever undertaken in Britain"*. Delays, a builders' strike and shortages of materials, all conjoined to send debts spiralling into the stratosphere. By 1977 they totalled £4 million. For the next four years, Chelsea had no money to buy a single new player. Hooliganism raised its ugly face on the terraces leading to Chelsea fans being subjected to a ban for away matches in 1977.

Chelsea entered a period of acute uncertainty and disappointment.

With all the furore, what would 1975/76 bring on the field in Division Two? A flicker of hope died after two successive 3-1 victories early on turned out to be a flash in the pan, and 7 draws

and 2 losses saw the season out in miserable style. It could have been worse though, and with the team on 11th place, McCreadie had stopped the club from haemorrhaging.

Ray Wilkins in midfield was top goalscorer with 12 that season, which was a sure sign of a rather sad situation out on the field.

As the 1976/77 season progressed, it was clear that McCreadie might do even better than just stop the rot. Dempsey and Hutchinson were no longer in blue, but just two losses in 13 matches got the team off to a cracking start and sent them to the top of the table where they stayed for most of the season. McCreadie motivated his men to focus and hustle for the ball, and they ran forward to success. It was balm to soothe the soul of everyone who wanted Chelsea to succeed. Pipped at the post by Wolverhampton Wanderers, Chelsea came

home second at the end of the season, and the fright was over as they celebrated promotion. Honours went to young striker Steve Finnieston who popped home 24 goals for his team. Ray Wilkinson, praised by Charlie Cooke for his *"skill, technique and finishing ability"*, was another young player given his head by Suart, who proved his worth under McCreadie.

And just as it seemed that a corner had been turned, another spat when Chelsea needed it least, ruined the prospects of the club. McCreadie abruptly departed, ostensibly over a contractual dispute, which Chinese whispers turned into problem over McCreadie's demands for a company car. This fresh crisis blew former right-back Ken Shellito into the manager's seat. He was doing brilliant work with the youth team graduates and did well in keeping Chelsea in Division

Arsenal V Chelsea Aerial combat 4th October 1976

One in 1977/78, a season that included a thrilling 4-2 FA Cup win over European champions Liverpool. But 14 defeats by Christmas including an appalling run of 6 defeats in a row in led Shellito to conclude that he was not the man for the job, and he handed in his resignation halfway through the 1978/79 season. Osgood returned briefly, but this was not a problem that one man could solve.

Shellito was succeeded by the legendary Danny Blanchflower, former Tottenham Hotspur captain and manager of Northern Ireland. There was a communication breakdown between the players and their new manager which was never resolved. Blanchflower also found the problems too great to handle, and the club vanished out of sight of the top clubs to land at the bottom of Division One. With just 20 points, it had been an appalling showing and a season to forget. Only five league games had been won, with 27 defeats charting the fall of a once mighty team.

To those who were still watching, it may have seemed that it would all get worse when Ray Wilkins was sold to Manchester United.

By September 1979, Blanchflower, too, was Chelsea history. In came the inexperienced hero from England's 1966 World Cup final win, Geoff Hurst, to replace him, with Bobby Gould as his assistant.

A promising start in the first four games was wiped out by four successive defeats. As if they had just been testing the fans' loyalty, immediately after that came 14 games with only three defeats. The Blues hit top spot and stayed there and looked certain to go up until 3 draws and two defeats in April 1980 sank them to 4th.

The sparkle proved to be short-lived and faded away. In 1980/81 the team struggled to find any consistent form. Unable to win their first 7 games, they then lost just one of the next 16 before stumbling again. They dropped to 20th, had a meteoric rise to second and finally fell away to 12th. It was the end of Hurst, who was sacked in an atmosphere of rancour with one year of his three-year contract still to run.

Chelsea were left rudderless for a few games until John Neal was appointed manager. He had left Middlesbrough under a cloud having been involved in a boardroom dispute there.

The supporters were prepared for anything by this time but desperately longing for the stability that would bring results. Two wins got the club off to a good start and everyone breathed a sigh of relief; rather too quickly, because there was a rapid fall to 14th. Neal and the team were soon able to soothe the pain of the hammering they received from Rotherham, 6-0, by delivering 13 games without defeat. Clive Walker with 17 and Alan Mayes with 16 goals helped stem the descent down the league so that when the last fan had left the ground after a 1-1 draw with Blackburn Rovers on the 15th May 1982, the Blues were on 12th place again and relegation fears had been banished for the summer at least.

The problem was how to improve the quality of the team without any serious money to buy players. Neal knew what players he wanted for the money available to him and got them; David Speedie from Darlington was one of them. *"Neal", said Ken Bates the new Chelsea chairman, who bought the club that year, "was one of the best managers".*

Now all he had to do was prove it.

He did. But unfortunately not before he was hit by the Chelsea curse. In 1982/83 the Chelsea ship almost went belly up. 12 goals scored by Mike Fillery, a midfielder, made him the highest scoring player. Hardly the way to challenge for a title. The way to get relegated in fact and they almost managed that, too. 18th position gave everyone a mighty scare.

In 1983/84, out of the blue, the magic was back. Neal had found a winning combination in his three forwards David Speedie, Pat Nevin and Kerry Dixon. Three talented players who were eternally at odds with one another personally and often on the field. The antagonism — Nevin is quoted as saying of his Scottish team-mate, Speedie, *"We absolutely despised each other"* — was, perhaps, motivating, because on the field the three forwards were scintillating. Their ball skills had the fans in raptures and the goals came for all three, Dixon finding the net 34 times with Nevin on 14 and Speedie on 13.

The season started with a walloping for Derby County 5-0 and a sensational 17-game run without defeat started on January the 14th 1984, which included another 5-0 walloping, this time of rivals Leeds United. The team played swift, attacking football, the best seen at Stamford Bridge in many years. Chelsea sailed to the top of the division and there they stayed. Neal had guided them away from the horror of Division Three and up to become Second Division champions.

When the Blues finished 6th in their first season back with the big boys, it was as though they had never been away. Kerry Dixon fired in the goals as though his opponents were the same as the season before; 36 left his boot, with Speedie knocking in another 16.

Neal suffered from heart problems and was finally forced to relinquish the managership. Assistant John Hollins took over. Fortunately he proved a to be steady hand.

The trio of Chelsea forwards did it again in 1985/86, shooting Chelsea into another 6th place. Along the way, fans enjoyed Manchester City falling to the blue onslaught twice, Arsenal beaten 2-1, and could then wince at a 6-1 slapping at the hands of Queens Park Rangers.

The team was flashing along in the League Cup, too, getting as far as the semi-finals where the Blues met Sunderland. Sunderland came out on top, leading to fans almost causing a riot. Mounted police and supporters spread out over the pitch and later onto the streets.

But like Icarus flying too close to the sun, Chelsea lost momentum.

Hollins and his assistant Ernie Walley became embroiled in arguments with some of the players, Speedie and Spackman to name just two, who paid the price by being sold. The whole team suffered, and the dramatic rise was followed by a dramatic fall. Dixon did his best but 11 goals was not going to stop the decay. Speedie hit just 4, a sure sign that something was badly out of kilter. The lightness had left Stamford Bridge. The Blues were 14th.

The next season, the headaches began once more. Hollins lost his

Pat Jennings Arsenal keeper in aerial battle with Kerry Dixon 25th August 1984

job in March 1988. He was succeeded by Bobby Cambell. Nothing could be done. A play-off system was then in place and Chelsea lost out to Middlesbrough, which again led to crowd trouble with fans attempting a pitch invasion,

The team still had talent. It was internal warfare that was doing the damage. 18th position and relegation was the reward.

The season of 1988/89 came around. The opening could hardly have been worse if the team had tried to lose. 8 games with just one win, and 4 losses. Campbell looked set to follow Hollins. But overnight, after the 4-1 defeat by Scunthorpe in the Littlewoods Cup on the 27th of September, a team with a new spirit popped up. Dixon and fellow forward Gordon Durie were in the mood for goals and

brought their final tallies to 26 and 17 respectively. Central defender Graham Roberts struck 12 penalties on his way to 15 goals. There were just 4 more lost games for the remainder of the season. Walsall vanished beneath a 7-goal blue wave. Manchester City crumpled, and Leeds United went down 1-0. Chelsea became unstoppable, racing ahead to gain 99 points, ahead of nearest rivals Manchester City by 17 points. This astonishing revival won them promotion once again.

No one could know at the time, but the nail-biting see-sawing between divisions was now a thing of the past and the real glory years full of....

....thrills and excitement awaited

the patient supporters.

Division One Micky Hazard goes in brave 4th October 1985

David Speedie takes on Sunderland 27th August 1984

THE FUTURE BEGINS

 nly the Charity Shield came their way the next season, and even that was a draw, 1-1, against Manchester United. Liverpool were saved by a John Barnes' penalty kick.

It was 1989, when Campbell watched his team play on the grass at Wimbledon for their first match, and come out 1-0 on top. The win heralded a good season which might have been spectacular had two attacks of the old weakness not interfered. The first attack

Kerry Dixon 1991-1992 season

spiked the joy in December; a 5-2 home defeat to Wimbledon, a 4-2 defeat at Queens Park and another 5-2 defeat at home to Liverpool. The second hiccup struck at the end of January 1990 when a 3-1 defeat by Bristol City in the FA Cup was the precursor to another three defeats in a row. Nonetheless, the lads rallied by the middle of February and it was a very good first season in the top division, which ended with the club placed 5th. Chelsea were denied a UEFA Cup place when league runners-up Aston Villa took the only spot allotted to English clubs. There was, however, the Full Members Cup to enjoy which brought a 1-0 win against Middlesbrough at Wembley. A taste of things to come. The season had been a testimony to Campbell's ability; a largely unremarkable team — the exceptional Kerry Dixon was still sparking and hit 22 goals — had been moulded into a team to be reckoned with.

At last some serious money was available again, and two midfielders, Dennis Wise and Andy Townsend, became the first million-pound recruits to the club.

The manager had less success the following season, 1990/91. It was the first of six that found Chelsea uninspired in the middle of the table. The statistics at the close of the 1995/96 season tell the tale; 11th place 4 times, 14th place twice. The team was lacklustre, and individual skills that could raise the team above mediocrity were in short supply.

Bobby Cambell was promoted at the end of the 1990/91 season and took up the job of general manager, replaced as first-team manager by Ian Porterfield, who had been first team coach. It was not one of the most successful transitions the club had endured, as the first of those 14th positions, in 1991/92, proved. Only Dennis Wise got past double figures in front of the goal, hitting 13, so the fans still had a few dry years to endure. Nigel Spackman had returned in 1992 and summed up his assessment of the poor performances with the words, " … the lunatics were running the asylum".

Another season of change followed. The 1992/93 season was the first for Chelsea in the newly-formed Premier League, which had been created in February of 1992 by the top clubs so that they could take advantage of lucrative payments by television companies in exchange for match rights. Managing director Colin Hutchinson was convinced that Ian Porterfield had to go and sacked the manager midway through the season, which was one of those that opened and closed with defeats. A terrible run of 13 games without a win finally put an end to the manager's post for Porterfield. His successor was 1970s cup hero David Webb, even though Bates was not sure that Webb could handle the situation. Webb took on the job as caretaker manager for the remainder of the season, did what was needed and was able to staunch the bloodletting, preventing possible disaster; an achievement not to be scorned, as he lifted the club from 15th to 11th. Webb had instigated much-needed change to squash the 'cliquey' and 'unmanageable' atmosphere prevailing in the Chelsea dressing room at the time. *"He really saved Chelsea"*, said Spackman.

The era of Glenn Hoddle dawned. The 35 year-old took over and began the changes that were to bring Chelsea to where they longed to be; playing for honours. It was a hard road to travel, and the fruits of Hoddle's labours would not ripen for several years.

Hoddle was determined to introduce a 3-5-2 system, whereas the players had become used to the 4-2-2 lineup, and the changeover did not produce success, which made Hoddle's job psychologically difficult for him. Initially, in fact, the team began to sink again in 1993/94. A long run of defeats started in October, six in a row, which left them in the relegation zone on 21st place.

An angry captain, Denis Wise, confronted his players after a 3-1 defeat to Southampton on December the 28th 1993. Tension clouded his relationship with them after that, but the very next day the team changed direction and beat Newcastle United 1-0 to end the decay. 14th position was more than anyone had expected earlier in the season.

Hoddle had scored 5 times. Mark Stein managed 11, and it

Chelsea V Luton Fc Fa Cup Semi-Final 9th April 1994

was evident that he was operating at a level far below what was expected of him. Yet Hoddle could see the light at the end of the long tunnel. A great FA Cup run had led to the final, although a 4-0 defeat at the hands of Manchester United showed how much was still to be done at Stamford Bridge.

1994/95. Hoddle stuck to his guns but had to halt a slow slide with a 6-game undefeated run in April, just in time to heave the team back up to 11th place. An uneventful season, apart from the fact that lifelong fan, billionaire Matthew Harding, joined club's board in 1994, and Chelsea began their battle in the Cup Winner's Cup where they reached the semi-final. Real Zaragoza were the better side,

winning 3-2 on aggregate, but it was a creditable run for the Blues in the state they were in at the time. And a vital decision was made by Hoddle, Harding and Hutchinson in May 1995 to try and secure Ruud Gullit for the club.

Harding's enthusiasm led to him investing £26.5 million in the club, and with that money a bid was made for Gullit's services. The Dutchman was soon pulling on the blue no. 4 shirt.

Another international name became blue in the 1995/96 season; defender/midfielder Dan Petrescu from Romania. Mark Hughes also signed on, from Manchester United. These three were not enough to take the team above another disappointing 11th place although the

Dennis Wise and Gianluca Vialli Celebrate with the FA Cup 17th May 1997

omens were good; form had been quite consistent and the Chelsea style of football had evolved again into a game that flowed and where passes were swift; and the team had made their way through to the FA Cup semi-final, which had ended in a 2-1 defeat against Manchester United.

Gullit, however, had been a revelation, and the man twice voted World Soccer Player of the Year was already being talked about as the best player ever to wear a Chelsea shirt. It took a while for him to adjust to the Hoddle method and the manager's desire for Gullit to perform his genius in midfield. Gullit was still worth his weight in gold and was runner up to Eric Cantona as Player of the Year.

On the 2nd May 1996, Hoddle left Chelsea to take up the manager's reigns for the England squad. It was a difficult moment, and the wrong decision about a new manager could have dire consequences. There was absolutely no doubt about the fans' choice. It was Rudi Gullit's name that echoed around Stamford Bridge from tens of thousands of throats. And what a choice it turned out to be. Gullit asked Graham Rix to leave his youth team manager position and be his assistant. A good choice.

In the team, in a season that was going to set supporters' heart

Gianfranco Zola holding off Everton's David Unsworth and Slaven Bilić 27th July 1997

54

The Chelsea Team Celebrate winning the 1998 UEFA Cup Winners Cup

on fire, was forward Gianfranco Zola, a future Chelsea star whom another legend, Alex Ferguson, described as *"… a clever little so-and-so"*. Praise indeed from the great man. Zola was to provide Chelsea fans with blissful moments of brilliant skill.

Gullit launched into his first season in fine style, and for a brief period, the club bounced between 2nd and 3rd in the table. French defender Frank Leboeuf had followed Gullit's siren call and Zola, Mark Hughes and another new signing, Italian Gianluca Vialli, all went over the ten goals apiece marker and helped the club stay two-thirds of the way up the table and better, all season. By the end of the season Gullit had brought them onto 6th position and proven his worth. It was the highest placing since 1990 and an impressive start. The Blues were becoming a team that other managers had to be wary of. But by the time the Blues won their last match of the season away at Everton, 1-2, the club was in a state of excitement because Chelsea had fought their way through to the FA Cup final. There had been a dramatic win against Liverpool to savour along the way. Mark Hughes had inspired a 4-2 victory after Chelsea had entered the second half 2-0 down.

The club was truly an international gathering place when the 116th Cup final, Chelsea against Middlesbrough, got under way; Canada, Italy, Romania, France and Norway were all represented in the Chelsea team as well as England, Scotland and Wales. And a Dutch manager, of course. Hutchinson once famously described the club as *" … a continental club playing in England"*.

The drama happened almost as soon as the game began. Di Matteo found himself with space and when the ball was at his feet having got there via Steve Clarke and Dennis Wise, he thought, *" … maybe I will shoot"*. He unleashed a drive from 25 yards that had the ball dipping down behind the Middlesbrough goalie and into the net after just 43 seconds. The score was unchanged as the first half ended after a Gianluca Festa goal for Middlesbrough was ruled offside. Chelsea dominated a game that did little to thrill except when, 7 minutes from time, Zola flicked the ball to the boot of Chelsea midfielder, Eddie Newton and from there it hit the back of the Middlesbrough net again. Chelsea had made it. Having been elsewhere since 1970, the Cup had

found its way back to Stamford Bridge.

Sadly, the man whose love for the club had set the whole dream in motion was not at Wembley to feel the pride that others did on that wonderful day. Matthew Harding had died in a helicopter accident transporting him home from a match a few months earlier. Without his injection of money, Chelsea may well have remained a middle-ranking club fated to remain just outside of the realm of the big hitters.

Gullit had a keen eye for talent, and he soon had Gustavo Poyet, and Norwegian Tore André Flo under contract, together with

Celestine Babayaro, Graeme Le Saux and Ed de Goey. It was an impressive haul.

It was natural that expectations were high all round as the 1997/98 season began. Flo and Vialli found the net 13 times each with Mark Hughes just one short on 12. By the middle of the season, Chelsea were contending for the top spot. It was an exciting time. But anyone who knew Chelsea history would not have been surprised at what happened next. Gullit started to lose control of the players and his own judgement. Perhaps he was too inexperienced, perhaps the burden of being a player-coach was too great. With

Cup Winners Cup final Gianluca Vialli & Dennis Wise celebrate Chelsea's victory with trophy 19th May 1998

the team flying high in the league and two cup challenges running smoothly, the UEFA Cup Winner's Cup and the League Cup, the unwanted crunch came after a 3-1 defeat to Everton in January 1998. A dispute with the board was the official version, although this version is disputed by Gullit. Whatever the real cause, the axe fell swiftly. Another player took over. Gianluca Vialli. Hutchinson wanted to appoint someone who knew the line the management had taken and would continue it so as to avoid disruption, if possible. There

was a wobble in the league with 4 lost games. The team pulled itself back together and landed on 4th spot.

That was not the real story of the season.

In the League Cup, the Blues gave that season's League Champions Arsenal a 3-1 hiding, a game to remember, and they went on to lift the Cup in the final beating Middlesbrough once more, 2-0.

Frank Leboeuf takes on Mustafa Izzet of Leicester City 1998

Lee Dixon of Arsenal tackles Roberto Di Matteo 31st January 1999

And there was still more.

In Europe, Vfb Stuttgart from Germany were lined up against Chelsea, who were to play in the UEFA European Cup Winner's Cup final in the Blues' last match of the season.

Zola was not on the field when the match started, due to a groin strain. Chelsea were described as being 'neat and inventive',

although the defences on both sides left a lot to be desired and could take no real credit for the 0-0 half-time scoreline.

Seventy minutes passed, and the play moved back and forth without result until Vialli took the decision to play Zola after all. Zola had been on the field for just 30 seconds when Dennis Wise tucked the ball into a space on Chelsea's left and Zola streaked after it past the German backs towards the Stuttgart box. The goalie was off his line, but Zola was not going to let the chance pass him by. The ball fired from his right foot was unstoppable as it howled into the Stuttgart net. Even with ten men after Dan Petrescu was sent off, Chelsea were home and dry, the first English team to win the competition twice a wonderful ending to a dramatic season.

1998/99 started off with a whimper before the Blues powered upwards to make a serious bid for the league title, topping the table on four occasions. The UEFA Super Cup fell into Chelsea's hands in August, when they dispensed with Real Madrid 1-0 after a Gus Poyet goal. Vialli's team became the first English side to be

composed solely of foreign-born players, in a game that had become increasingly globalised. Only four league games were lost as the Blues drew up four points short of Manchester United on third place.

There was great promise in this exciting team. Yet for much of the 1999/2000 season, the team were not serious contenders for the league title, dropping to 10th at one point before embarking on a long pull back to finish 5th. Tore André Flo with 19 goals and Gus Poyet with 18, had not shirked their responsibilities, but 59 goals conceded had taken their toll. Consolation that year came in the form of a rather uninspiring 1-0 FA Cup final win against Aston

Gustavo Poyet beats Shay Given to score winning goal FA CUP Semi-Final Wembley 9th April 2000

John Terry tracks Thierry Henry in FA Cup 4th round cup tie 18th February 2001

Villa, which only highlighted the fact that the team needed to be rejuvenated; new faces were called for. There had been Champions League excitement along the way, though, with a blistering 5-0 win against Turkish side Galatasaray and a momentous 3-1 blasting of Barcelona.

But there were reports, too, that Vialli was having difficulties and that various tensions were running unchecked between some players and their manager. Vialli made a valuable purchase in the shape of Dutchman Jimmy Floyd Hasselbaink, but even his presence and a win in the Charity Shield against Manchester United in August 2000 together with a 4-2 win against West Ham to start the 2000/2001 season could not dispel the cloud hovering above Vialli. 2 league wins was all he had to show from 9 matches by the end of September. Vialli did not watch the 9th, because he had already been abruptly sacked. It was a sad end for a man who, disregarding whatever other faults he had, had overseen Chelsea's most thrilling, successful period ever. Chelsea got to the end of the season, settling on 6th place.

Graham Rix had taken over on a temporary basis, and Hutchinson knew that it was time to set an experienced managerial hand on the tiller. *"It was time for rebuilding"*, he said, and he turned to Italian Claudio Ranieri who had won cups in both Italy and Spain and who had recently left Atlético Madrid.

As Ranieri could not speak English when he arrived, several of the players had to translate for him. His task was to rebuild the team with younger players, always a risk, and he spent more than £30 million doing so creating a new midfield grouping en route. In came the likes of Emmanuel Petit and Boudewijn Zenden. A few eyebrows were raised, however, when Denis Wise was released. Who could have foreseen, however, that when Frank Lampard arrived, perhaps the greatest Chelsea player of all time had entered the Chelsea fold.

Maybe it was due to his ability that despite his difficulties with the language, Ranieri helped the club hit 6th place again at the end of his first season in 2002 and not a lower one. Chelsea did reach the League Cup semi-finals and the FA Cup final, though, where

they went down 2-0 to Arsenal. Jimmy Floyd Hasselbaink had a great season, hitting 26 goals. Zola struck 12, Poyet 12, and Eiður Guðjohnsen 13.

Rumours had been circulating for a while that the club was experiencing financial difficulties, and these problems seemed to be confirmed by the fact that no new players were signed for the forthcoming season.

Now nicknamed 'The Tinkerman' because of his much-criticised habit of rotating the squad so often, Ranieri send the 2002/03 team out for what turned out to be one of the better seasons. 16 players got behind successful attempts at goal in games that brought a 4th place, although this separated them from league winners Manchester United by a considerable 16 points. There had been high points to celebrate, too, like the 5-0 walloping dished out to Manchester City, the 4-1 blitz on Everton and best of all, the Blues had sent Liverpool away smarting from a 2-1 defeat,

securing a Champions League place for themselves at the same time.

THE MIGHTY DUO

One of the most momentous changes in the club's tangled history was about to take place. The financial crisis came to a head that year, and Bates sold the club 'out of the blue', so to speak, for £60 million to an unknown Russian billionaire; Roman Abramovich. The new owner had soon eradicated the club's £80 million debt almost entirely and financed a whole raft of new signings, including Geremi Hernan Crespo, Joe Cole, Damien Duff, Glen Johnson and Claude Makélélé. It was the start of a fantasy come true.

2003/04 turned out to be Ranieri's last season for Chelsea, one which brought the club's best league performance for 49 years. There were four sequences of winning runs when there were 9, 10, 7 and 9 games without defeat. Newcastle were pounded 5-0, Watford 4-0 and Wolverhampton Wanderers 5-2 in an exciting title race spearheaded by the talent of Hasselbaink and his 17 goals. The managership was taken from Ranieri on May the 30th 2004 although he had consistently improved the team's strength. It may have been the lack of trophies or strange decisions taken during matches that sealed his fate under the new owner hungry for glory; the real reasons are unclear.

The man who followed him was to become perhaps the most famous of the Chelsea legends. José Mourinho. Another legend, Dutch scout Piet de Visser joined him, and Chelsea set out on the road to the top.

The season 2004/05 started without Hassalbaink but with Didier Drogba in the front line and Petr Čech between the posts. John Terry was Mourinho's captain, who led the Blues out to a terrific start with 8 wins in 10 games, which included a 3-1 UEFA Champions League win against Porto. They moved up to the number one spot after 12 matches and there they stayed until the end of the season. The scalps taken reveal the size of the achievement; Tottenham squashed 2-0 at White Hart Lane, Manchester United battered 3-1 at Old Trafford, and two glorious 4-2 defeats of Barcelona and Bayern Munich in the UEFA Champions League. In February, Chelsea won the League Cup in a nerve- tingling defeat of Liverpool, 3-2 in the final at the Millenium Stadium. Drogba had found the net 16 times that season and so had Norwegian Eiður Guðjohnsen. Lampard had risen to the top with 19.

The statistics show that Chelsea had won with the best points total, 95, — gained in a record-winning 29 undefeated outings — and best defensive record — just 15 conceded all season — in the history of the elite English leagues. Terry was voted PFA Player of the Year and Lampard became Footballer of the Year. The other main trophies evaded Mourinho's classy men, but silverware arrived in the shape of the Carling Cup, gained with a victory over Liverpool. What a way to celebrate 100 years of football at Stamford Bridge.

The pace was kept high in 2005/06 as the wins piled up from the outset, ten in an undefeated run of eleven premiership games. After a hiccup, a 1-0 loss to Manchester United away, they set off again for another ten premiership wins in a row. Their dominance in the table was so great that even losing the final two games did not stop them from raising the league title again for the second year running, a magnificent achievement. The 3-0 win over title rivals Manchester United at Stamford Bridge in April, was sweet compensation for those last two lost games. United manager Alex Ferguson confessed to being *"jealous" of the defensive qualities at Chelsea, and that their home record had been "sensational"*; praise indeed. Chelsea had hit the top spot after the third match and never gave it up. Lampard again had a superb year, hitting 20 goals, with Drogba not far behind on 16. The premiership win made Chelsea the first London club to gain successive league titles since the 1930s, the fifth side to do so since the end of WWII.

Their six clean sheets since the start of the season was a record, and they had drawn level with the Newcastle United squad of 1906/07 in having the best home record for a top division team, with 18 wins and 1 draw from 19 games.

The club that had been so often derided as no more than a

meeting place for trendy, artistic Londoners, had proven that they were capable of delivering the best football anywhere.

Amongst all the excitement, one piece of very sad news came in March 2006. The legendary Chelsea player Peter 'Ossie' Osgood died on the 1st. He had suffered a heart attack. His exceptional skill had enthralled all who had seen him, one of the most talented payers of his generation, and he remains a favourite son of the club to this day. His dedication to Chelsea was undiminished even after he retired from football, and his ashes were buried under the penalty spot at the shed end at Stamford Bridge. A statue of him was unveiled in 2010 outside the west stand.

During the summer of 2006, stars Eiður Guðjohnsen, William Gallas and Damien Duff left the club. But fresh impetus arrived in the shapes of Andriy Shevchenko, Michael Ballack and Ashley Cole, considered by some to be one of the best defenders of his generation

63

anywhere in the world. Evidently, Mourinho intended to continue delivering razor-sharp football.

After a brief period on the number one spot in 2006/07, the Blues spent the remainder of the season chasing the leaders. They were Manchester United who came home 6 points clear of Chelsea in 2007. There had been great football along the way. German midfielder Michael Ballack made an immediate impact and Drogba was in crackling form with 33 goals to his credit. Lampard, too, had a respectable 21.

There was a great deal to cheer about that season.

Although injuries made life as a supporter interesting, to say the least — there was a serious head injury to Petr Cech and injuries to John Terry, Ricardo Carvalho and Carlo Cudicini, leading Mourinho to say that he was involved in *"survival football"* — the Blues suffered just 3 defeats in the league, to Middlesbrough, Tottenham and Liverpool. There was a run of 11 games undefeated, and the trophies

came, too. The League Cup was in the Blues' hands after Arsenal went down 2-1, and the FA Cup run ended in an even greater triumph as Manchester United, who had snatched the League title from Chelsea, were defeated 1-0 at Wembley. By chance, Chelsea was the last team to win the Cup at the old Wembley Stadium.

At the height of success, the antagonisms within the club that surfaced almost as regularly as a full moon, when all was well on the field, returned. Mourinho and Abramovich had been in open conflict for months by the time the 2007/08 season got underway, and in September 2007, 'mutual consent' saw a parting of the ways.

"I can only say positive things about him", Mourinho had said of Abramovich just a short time before. There was also no doubt in his mind about his own abilities: *"If Roman Abramovich helped me out in training we would be bottom of the league, and if I had to work in his world of big business, we would be bankrupt!"*

Fans were bereft as Chelsea's finest manager, undefeated at home and with six trophies under his belt, left Stamford Bridge, joining FC Internazionale Milano, or Inter Milan as they are known outside Italy, in

John Terry (Capt) and Team Mates Celebrate with the Premier League Trophy 2005/06

June 2008.

Director of football at the London club, Avram Grant, was appointed as the new supremo. It would be difficult to fill Mourinho's shoes.

Mourinho's last season had started with a 3—2 Premier League defeat of Birmingham City to set a new record of 64 consecutive home league matches without defeat. Yet despite challenging strongly for the trophies, there was ultimately disappointment on all fronts, as the club were runners-up in the Premier League — 2 points behind Manchester United — the Football League Cup and the European Champions Cup. Was this what life without the colourful José would be like?

The board were not happy and Grant lost his job at the end of the season which saw Chelsea become the highest-ranked club by UEFA. A testimony to their match-winning consistency.

In came Brazilian, Luiz Felipe Scolari, to try and recapture the Mourinho magic.

Until November the 30th 2008 and a 2-1 home defeat to Arsenal, it seemed that the Chelsea league challenge would be as strong as ever. Chelsea had been riding on top, but after that defeat they could never regain the number one position.

Chelsea V Wycombe Wanderers Frank Lampard in action 23rd January 2007

Scolari's was a short-lived appointment, and he was given his marching orders on February the 9th, 2009 when results and performances were deemed to be 'deteriorating'.

Now it was the turn of Guus Hiddink to see what he could do. The Dutchman's presence brought immediate results and although he could not bring home the Premiership title — Chelsea finished 3rd — even though Anelka and Lampard had scored 45 goals between them, there was a thrilling run to the UEFA Champions League semi-final. Sadly it was lost to Barcelona on the replay with a controversial 1-1 draw, Barcelona scoring in stoppage time, after a 0-0 draw in Spain.

Still, there was to be a final attempt to salvage some glitter from the season. The FA Cup final was once again to see Chelsea compete for glory. This time against Everton. And the Blues delivered the performances the fans wanted to see, taking home the FA Cup for the second time in three years with a Lampard-Drogba 2-1 victory.

Hiddink had become a hugely popular figure at the Bridge but had promised not to abandon the Russian national team, so he handed over to former A.C Milan coach Carlo Ancelotti for 2009/10.

Fans' fears about the new manager were calmed after Manchester United were beaten on penalties in the Community Shield — the first time Chelsea had won a penalty shoot-out since 1998 — and then roared off to 6 consecutive wins in the league. But who could tell that it was going to be an incredible ride that season?

The Blues hit the top of the table and stuck to it for a long period. The competition was intense with Manchester United on their heels

Didier Drogba gets between Armand Traoré and Philippe Senderos 25th February 2007

and Arsenal challenging hard, too. There were slip-ups leading to Chelsea being knocked off the perch into second place after a loss to Wigan Athletic, 3-1. But Manchester were tamed in November, 1-0, and Arsenal were taught a lesson with a 3-0 defeat at Highbury. It was a magnificent season for Didier Drogba, busily cracking home the 37 goals that would make him top goalscorer. The goals came rushing in; five 3-0 victories, four 4-0 victories including Atletico Madrid, an 8-0 revenge thrashing of Wigan Athletic, 7-0 against Stoke City, 7-1 against Aston Villa, 7-2 against Sunderland, 5-0 against Portsmouth and Blackburn Rovers; there were stunning displays of world-class football. Chelsea were the first club to score 100 in a single season in the Premier League and with the final tally at 103, scored the second

highest number of goals in a season, behind Tottenham Hotspur with 111 in 1962/63. Those goals brought Chelsea back to the top of the Premier League and this time they were not to be dislodged. The reward was the third Premier League title in six years.

On May 15th, 2010, the Blues went out for their last game of the season against Portsmouth in the FA Cup final. The men in blue were up to the job, and with a goal from Drogba, Chelsea secured their first league/cup double. It had been an exceptional, a thrilling year. They had come a long way since the early days when greyhounds used to hurtle around the Stamford Bridge ground when no matches were being played.

Almost as though life was too good, the next season started with

Carling Cup Final José Mourinho celebrates with the cup 25th February 2007

67

a loss and ended with a loss, an uncomfortable echo of the bad old see-saw days; 1-3 against Manchester in the FA Community Shield to start and 1-0 against Everton in the Premier League to finish. In between those matches was a litany of misses. Recovering from the Community Shield loss the team delivered two 6-0 wins and top position, until a 1-0 defeat at Birmingham City in November started the decay. Buying David Luiz and Fernando Torres did not bring the glory back. Chelsea sank to fifth at one stage but fought their way back up to 2nd at the end of the season. It was all they could do. No FA Cup, no League Cup; no trophies at all, in fact.

That fact was Ancelotti's death knell. He was dismissed after the last match, and André Villas-Boas became the new Chelsea manager for the 2011/12 season. Those who had hoped for continuity were disappointed even though the year began well enough; 10 games, one defeat to Manchester United 3-1 in the league but a 5-0 hiding given out to RC Genk in the UEFA Champions League tie.

Slowly but surely, however, the games began to slip from the team's grasp, and Villa-Boas did not last the season. He was sacked on March the 1st following a 1-0 defeat to West Bromwich Albion, which left him with a win percentage of less than 50%; the first time that Abramovich had had that experience since he had taken over at the club. Roberto di Matteo filled the gap as caretaker manager. The team's form did not improve greatly in the league as the final sixth place — and just 13 and 16 goals respectively for Drogba and Lampard — testifies. The excitement was to be found in the other competitions.

UEFA Champions League final celebrations 19th May 2012

The FA Cup run was going well. Portsmouth were downed with a 4-0 win, Leicester vanished 5-2 and Tottenham 5-1, before a Liverpool-Chelsea meeting in the final. And the struggle went to the Blues. They were the better team for sixty minutes, but it was thanks to an heroic save by Petr Čech that denied Liverpool an equaliser, that the Blues carried the day with a 2-1 victory, the seventh time they had lifted the trophy. The fourth time in six seasons.

There was more to come just six days later.

Chelsea had worked their way to the UEFA Champions League final after sending Benfica and holders Barcelona home defeated, to set up a meeting with mighty Bayern Munich. The Germans took the lead in the 83rd minute. Drogba headed in the equaliser. Petr Cech saved a penalty and after extra time, the resulting shoot-out was a gruelling test of nerves. The Germans went in front 3-1. Cech proved

his worth once again with 2 saves to keep Chelsea hopes alive. Chelsea drew level, and it was fitting that Drogba should be the one to hit the winning goal that saw Chelsea hold the first UEFA Champions League title in their history. It was a magnificent achievement and, perhaps, Chelsea's finest hour.

Di Matteo had pulled the iron out of the fire, but hero worship can vanish overnight and in di Matteo's case, the adoration ended abruptly in November 2012. An eight-game winning run came to end at home against Manchester United, 2-3. A cardinal sin had been committed, losing at home, and Abramovich was unforgiving. Rafael Benitez came to Stamford Bridge, one of the most unpopular choices ever made. His connection with Liverpool and remarks he had made about Chelsea ensured that he was not welcomed by many Chelsea fans, and his reception during the match with Manchester City on the

69

The ball hits the back of the Spurs net as Costa's deflected shot puts Chelsea a 2-0 up in the League Cup Final 1st March 2015

25th of November was described as, 'fiercely hostile'.

This season was without the Lampard-Drogba duo that had sustained so many victories. Drogba had moved on, but Lampard was still roaming with regulars Juan Mata and Fernando Torres to create chances in front of the goalmouth. Mata netted 20 and Torres 22 this season with Lampard on 17.

The team dipped down to fourth, bouncing between there and third place.

There was a mixture of results under Benitez. A 2-1 FA Cup defeat to Manchester City 2-1 at home did not go down well. A great UEFA Europa League run made fans happy. Winning the UEFA Europa League against old rivals Benfica, 2-1, made them even happier. Chelsea are the first side in history to hold two major European titles simultaneously and have won all three of UEFA's major club competitions, the only British club to have achieved this. Seven games undefeated to end the season put them in 3rd place, which at least meant Champions League qualification. With so much swapping of managers it was hard to see what the true potential of the team really was. The Chelsea directors decided that whatever the potential, Benitez was not the man to carry it forward to success. He left at the end of the 2013 season, in June.

Then there was an extraordinary announcement to delight fans after the comings and goings of the previous years. The new supremo was to be none other than José Mourinho. It is unusual for a manager to be allowed, or even want to return to a club that he has managed before. It shows the esteem in which he is held that Abramovich decided to let bygones be bygones and have one of the most talented managers in the game return to have another go at glory. It also shows the affection with which Mourinho looks at Chelsea, where he won so much football glory. *"In my career I've had two great passions",* said Mourinho on his return to the Blues, *"Inter and Chelsea — and Chelsea is more than important for me".*

Confidence was high with Mourinho back in the driving seat and

claiming that he was now more mature than when he had left in 2007.

However, the season did not go as planned.

There were no cups to celebrate, after the loss to Bayern Munich on a penalty shoot-out in the UEFA Super Cup and the 1-2 home defeat against FC Basel in the UEFA Champions League. And although a run of nine games undefeated began on the 21st September and cheered everyone's hearts, it was a false dawn. Defeats began to pepper the score lines until a second run, undefeated in twelve games this time, brought them into the February of 2014 in good spirits. They had every reason to be happy, having become the first team in the Premier League to beat Manchester City, at the Etihad Stadium on the 3rd, 0-1, (although they went down to them 2-0 in the FA Cup on the 15th). By the end of that month Chelsea were back at the top of the Premiership.

But losses began to tarnish the glow. The terrific unbeaten home record that Mourinho's team had established collapsed on the 19th of April when Sunderland downed Chelsea 1—2. The Blues were also pushed out of the Champions League in the second leg of the semi-finals, going down to Atlético, 1—3.

But the blue danger was ever present. Having slipped from the number 1 spot in the Premier League, Chelsea edged closer to leaders Liverpool after giving them a hiding in Liverpool, 0—2. It was the draw at home to Norwich that plunged the sword into Chelsea's hopes. The thirteen losses that season had proven to be too great a burden to carry, and the team ended on third place behind their two Manchester rivals.

Not a reason to be downhearted. The team had shown its teeth, after all. Next season would bring the results everyone hoped for.

Triumphant, Turbulent Times.

The previous season had shown what Chelsea and Mourinho were capable of, and although Ashley Cole left in July after eight years in

Chelsea blue and Romelu Lukaku also went his way, Didier Drogba was back on a one-year deal to delight fans and Atlético Madrid striker Diego Costa was also coming to town.

And Costa — who became top goalscorer with 21 goals — opened the scoring that season to bring the side level in the match with Burnley in the season opener, which the Blues then won, 1-3. It was a good omen, and just four losses throughout the season showed the form that the team had reached. The other big boys were made to tremble as Chelsea catapulted themselves to the top from the very start; and there they stayed for the entire season. Everton were completely demolished, 3-6 in August, Manchester United were held

to a draw before being beaten 1-0 later in the season and Manchester City were tied down to two, 1-1 draws.

There had been a whopping 6-0 defeat of NK Maribor in the UEFA Champions League on the 21st of October to delight the crowd, and on the 25th of November in the same competition, Chelsea went home victorious against Schalke 04, 0-5. Memories to savour — let's sweep the 5-3 defeat to Tottenham Hotspur on the 1st of January 2015 under the carpet!

The season was notable for the actions of a Chelsea hero, John Terry, who broke the record for the most goals by a defender in Premier League history after sending in the equaliser at Liverpool

Pedro scores his second during the Premier League match against AFC Bournemouth at Stamford Bridge on 26th December 2016

in the 1-1 draw in May. And Eden Hazard became the only player in Europe to take more than 15 penalties and strike all of them home. This was a team to be proud of.

For his efforts, Mourinho took home the Premier League Manager of the Season and LMA Manager of the Year awards.

So, with 87 points to Manchester City's 79, Chelsea were the Premier League winners once more. They had also won the League Cup in March 2015 seeing off Tottenham Hotspur 2-0. It did not seem unreasonable to expect that the team could now consolidate their obvious talents and dominate the next season, too.

There was nothing to suggest there was trouble in the air as the 2015/16 season got underway. True, it hurt when the club let the legendary goalkeeper Petr Čech leave for three years to join London rivals Arsenal; Bosnian goalkeeper Asmir Begović came in July from Stoke City and made 17 appearances that season.

There was a warning shot across the bows, however, in the 2015 FA Community Shield, which Chelsea conceded 1—0 to Arsenal. Arsène Wenger had the added joy of defeating Mourinho for the first time in 14 games.

Then, disaster struck with just one win in five games, with Everton, Crystal Palace and Manchester City taking bites out of the Blues. By the end of August they were in 13th position. Gone the optimism of a few weeks previously. By the end of September they were 15th. The malaise seemed to have become chronic. In October they won just one game out of six; against Aston Villa, 2-0; at least that.

Something was badly awry, and by the 17th of December, Chelsea had lost nine out of sixteen league games. Anger and pressure were building; and then what had seemed unthinkable just months before became reality. Manager José Mourinho was sacked. This could only unsettle the players even further in the middle of a tough season.

The reigns were handed over to Dutchman Guus Hiddink for the remainder of the fixtures, whilst the club held its breath fearing an horrific dive to the bottom.

It didn't happen.

Neither did a spectacular resurrection. Sadly.

But what did happen was enough to save everyone's blushes. Hiddink managed to steady the ship, and more than earn his keep. Until March of the following year, there was just one loss in a sea of uncertain performances, a wodge of drawn games. But there was a joyous 5-1 thrashing of Manchester City in the FA Cup to revive faint hearts. The Blues still had it in them. No silverware there this time, though; the FA Cup dream vanished at Everton, a 2-0 loss in the 6th round.

City came back to take a 0-3 chunk out of the Blues towards the end of the season, but for Chelsea to finish 10th was a miracle, and much was owed to Hiddink for stopping the rot.

True, it was the lowest finish in the Premier League since the 1995—96 season for Chelsea, but the complaints were subdued; if Mourinho had stayed, who knows what might have happened. (Shudder and move on quickly.)

So. Some mighty and bold rethinking had been needed to provide the club with a manager who would be worthy of the job. Eyes alighted on a man, not without controversy, but who had brought Juventus to the giddy heights of success; the Italian Antonio Conte. On the 4th April 2016, he was confirmed as the new Chelsea manager.

Before the season started, Willian da Silva signed a new contract and N'Golo Kanté came from Leicester City.

A dash of cold water was applied when Chelsea lost their first pre-season match against Rapid Wien, 2-0, but with a few follow-up wins under their belts, they set off into the unknown again, for their 25th season in the Premier League.

With all eyes on the new manager, the fans were able to witness the Blues shoot away to a five-game undefeated start, only to flag slightly wth two losses back-to-back in September: 1-2 to Liverpool and 3-0 to Arsenal. Which was an unequivocal warning from the two big boys. A warning Chelsea took to heart, because they brought in thirteen wins in the next thirteen matches, gloriously taking out Manchester United 4-0 and Everton 5-0.

On the 26th of December 2016, Chelsea celebrated an all-time record of successive league victories. In a 3-0 home win over AFC Bournemouth on the 26th of December, Chelsea earned their 12th consecutive league victory. The winger Pedro, plus a penalty from Eden Hazard did the trick.

In fact, they went on to make the total thirteen consecutive victories, and only in January 2017 did the Blues lose concentration again and go down to Tottenham 0-2, as Conte made one of the rare miscalculations of his time at Chelsea and sent out a side ready for defence. Neither was Hazard at this best. A pity, but another match to consign to the blue bin. The good news was that anyone with a crystal ball would have been able to confirm that Chelsea would only slip up twice more. The bad news? Who has a crystal ball.

They put the defeat firmly behind them and turned in a run of eight games without a loss, holding an eager Liverpool team to a 1-1 draw in Liverpool and thumping Arsenal 3-1 in February at home.

The FA Cup run continued, too, and Manchester United were sent home with their tails between their legs in March after midfielder N'Golo Kanté chose the right moment to score his only Premiership goal with a low 51st-minute drive that got the better of United keeper David de Gea, who had skilfully thwarted both Hazard and Gary Cahill in the first half.

That win brought the lads into the FA Cup semi-final and another match against Tottenham; this time, they made sure the White Hart Lane boys knew who was in charge with a decisive 4-2 win at home. Willian, Hazard and Nemanja Matić put the game out of Tottenham's reach in a match that Tottenham had been confident they could win, as they were within four points of the Blues in the league.

Chelsea were in the cup final; and as chance would have it, the 2017 final was going to be an all-London affair; Arsenal had made it through as well.

Unfortunately, there was disappointment in the final, when an offside goal put Chelsea behind after just 4 minutes. Although Costa equalled the score on the 76th minute, Chelsea failed to keep out an Arsenal header on the 79th minute, and the cup was heading to Highbury.

The FA Cup semi-final win against Tottenham had been more than enough compensation for having lost against Manchester United, 2-0 in the league a few days before. That defeat, however, was to be the last the team would allow as they powered towards the league title with some best-of-the-season victories at home and away; both Everton and Middlesborough were dismissed, with three goals each for none against, and Watford fought hard in a spirited game only to be beaten 4-3. It had been an historic and emotional match for fans and players alike. John Terry celebrated his first league game since September 2016 by scoring Chelsea's 100th goal (and his 67th) in all competitions in the season after 22 minutes. It was only fitting that the legendary player should have played an important role in this terrific victory that gave the Blues their 6th league title. His decision to retire had not been taken lightly, and after such a long and illustrious career at the club where his heart was at home, it was always going to be tough to leave. It was the place where he had made "so many great memories and relationships, friends and managers … next week I'm going to be in bits, I know", he said in an interview after the match against Watford.

But after 492 appearances since John joined the first team in 1998, Chelsea finally had to say goodbye to one of its all-time legendary stars.

The final match of the season saw the team delight fans with the blue wave rolling over Sunderland adding a 5-1 victory to end a glorious league season on another positive note.

Diego Costa emerged as top goal scorer with 22 goals, giving Costa that honour for three consecutive seasons. Quite some achievement. In fact, only Bobby Tambling in the 1960s has been top goalscorer four times, but the seasons were not consecutive.

So this was an historic first for Chelsea and Diego Costa!

Whatever happens in the future, Chelsea's roller-coaster ride to the top of the world has been full of exciting players, brilliant footballing talent, high achievement and passionate characters on and off the field. Everyone involved with the blazing Blues has the determination to see that the Chelsea team always remains at the top of its game, fighting for the titles, exciting and entertaining, one of the greatest clubs in the history of English football.

75

Diego Costa of Chelsea celebrates winning the league following the Premier League match between Chelsea and Sunderland

THE PLAYERS

A list of the most famous players must inevitably be shorter than it should be and will always be disputed by the supporters of one player or another. But here are some of those who must grace every list.

GEORGE ROBERT MILLS

Mills was born on the 29th of December 1908 in Deptford and died on the 15th of July 1970. He came to Chelsea from Bromley as an amateur in 1929. The rest of his career was spent at the club. He was a prolific goalscorer, netting 125 goals in 239 games. Although more glamorous forwards such as Hughie Gallacher or Joe Bambrick hogged the limelight, Mills never wavered in his loyalty to the club.

Mills put away 14 goals in 20 games for Chelsea in his first season during their bid for promotion to Division One. In 1936/37 he hit 22 goals in 32 appearances and won three international caps, scoring a hat trick in a 5-1 win against Northern Ireland on the 23rd October 1937.

Mills is the eighth highest goal-scoring Chelsea player of all time, and his achievement in reaching 100 league goals made him the first Chelsea player to do so. Only five other players have equalled his scoring record. He became a coach at Chelsea when he retired as a player.

His later years were spent at a printing company in London, and he died in 1970 whilst on holiday in Torquay, Devon.

HUGHIE GALLACHER

Hugh Kilpatrick 'Hughie' Gallacher was born on the 2nd of February 1903 and died on the 11th of June 1957.

Gallacher was just 5' 5" tall, but his ball control was superb and he cunningly passed defenders to attack the goal with astounding striking power from either foot. He was a great all-rounder and could be found anywhere on the pitch. He scored 5 goals in one game on four separate occasions

A prolific goalscorer for the Scottish national team, he netted 23 goals from his 20 internationals with them, a ratio of more than one goal per

George Robert Mills
Hughie Gallacher.

game. He was in the Scottish team that humbled England in a 5-1 defeat at Wembley in the 1928 British Home Championship.

Gallacher's time at Chelsea was pitted with suspensions for indiscipline on the field, and off-the-field conflict. Bitter divorce proceedings saw him in the bankruptcy court in 1934.

Gallacher scored 463 times in 624 games.

Sadly, he fell victim to alcohol abuse. He was charged with cruelty to his son, and in Gateshead in 1957, he committed suicide by throwing himself in front of an express train.

VIVIAN JOHN WOODWARD

Woodward played as an amateur and was one of the greats of the early days of English football. A centre-forward, he scored 93 goals in 238 appearances for Tottenham and Chelsea. He was described as 'a master-model of team work', had a great ability for 'selling the dummy' and was considered the best header of his time.

At the international level, Woodward captained England and scored 29 goals in 23 matches, helping them to gold medals in the 1908 and 1912 Olympic games.

Woodward joined Chelsea in 1909 and scored 34 goals in 116 games, becoming the leading goalscorer in 1912/13 with 10 goals.

Woodward enlisted when WWI broke out, and served in the 17th Battalion of the Middlesex Regiment, a Footballers' Battalion. He saw action on the western front and was awarded the rank of captain. A hand grenade exploded near him during a battle in 1916 and injured him in the thigh. He later returned to France and survived the war.

When the journalist, Bruce Harris, visited Woodward in hospital towards the end of the former player's life, he noted Woodward was 'bedridden, paralysed, infirm beyond his seventy-four years'. A tragic end for a brave and talented man.

Woodward died in a nursing home on the 6th of February 1954.

ROY THOMAS FRANK BENTLEY

Bentley was born on the 17th of May 1924 and joined Chelsea in January 1948. He was one of the first deep-lying forwards, a tactic which

F. & J. SMITH'S CIGARETTES

77

Vivian John Woodward
Roy Thomas Frank Bentley

caused uncertainty in the opposition ranks. His form with Chelsea was inconsistent, but he was a powerful header and kicker of the ball in his 367 games for the club. He was chosen for the London XI in the Inter-Cities Fairs Cup and also capped 12 times in six years for England, becoming one of the English squad's top centre-forwards.

The highlight of his career at Chelsea was captaining the team in their first League title win in 1954/55. Bentley scored 150 goals in 367 appearances at Chelsea and was top scorer at the club during each of his eight full seasons spent there.

He ended his playing career with Queens's Park Rangers and later became a manager.

JAMES PETER 'JIMMY' GREAVES

Greaves was born in East Ham, London on the 20th of February 1940. He was one of the most talented forwards of his day, displaying calmness, and excellent balance and striking power. His goals were scored from almost every position in front of goal. Greaves signed as a junior in 1956, scoring a record 114 goals the following season for the Chelsea youth team. He was just 17 years old when he scored on his debut on 24th of August 1957 for Chelsea in a 1—1 draw against Tottenham Hotspur beginning a tradition of scoring in every debut until he retired in 1980.

Greaves married Irene in March 1958 at the age of 18.

He was Chelsea's top league goalscorer twice, in 1959 and 1961, and set a club record with 41 league goals in the 1960-61 season. He netted thirteen hat-tricks, and on three occasions, five goals and four goals. His hat-trick in November 1960 was scored when he was 20 years and 290 days old. It was his 100th league goal and with it he became the youngest player to pass the 100 goal mark; that record still stands.

Greaves was sold by Chelsea after the 1960/61 season although he wanted to remain at the club, and scored all four goals in his final game, when he was made captain, in a 4-3 victory over Nottingham Forest.

Greaves scored 366 league goals in 527 matches, 44 goals in international games; 410 in 584 games in total.

Greaves fought alcoholism, finally beating his addiction on the 28th of

Jimmy Greaves
Peter Bonetti

February 1978. He turned to television presenting as a football expert, notably in a partnership with Ian St. John in 'Saint and Greavsie', a popular Saturday lunchtime football show. He was also a football journalist and a host on many other television shows.

He suffered a mild stroke in February 2012 and had an operation on an artery in his neck.

PETER BONETTI

Bonetti was born on the 27th of September 1941 in Putney, London. The keeper was known as 'The Cat', because of his exceptional handling skills and lightning-fast reflexes. His specialty was a one-armed throw that could cover the distance of a drop kick.

Bonetti's first team debut came in 1960 and he was in the Chelsea youth side that won the FA Youth Cup. He was Chelsea's premier goalkeeper from the 1960/61 season on, and held that position more or less constantly for nineteen years.

The keeper's finest hour came in 1970 with two intense meetings with Leeds United for the FA Cup final. His courage and goalkeeping ability enabled Chelsea to get a 2-2 draw, and despite a Mick Jones tackle that badly injured his left knee in the second game, Bonetti played on with a non-functioning leg, denying the Leeds strikers any comfort in a 2-1 win for the Blues. Bonetti's performances that season led him to being voted runner-up in the FWA Footballer of the Year awards.

His final game for Chelsea was a 1—1 draw with Arsenal in May 1979 after a total of 729 appearances in nineteen years with more than 200 clean sheets. His career total is 628 matches.

Once his Chelsea career had ended, he lived on the Isle of Mull in Scotland and became a postman. Then followed a period of coaching with Chelsea, Manchester City and the England national side.

TERENCE FREDERICK 'TERRY' VENABLES

Venables, was born on the 6th of January 1943 in Dagenham.

Venables signed as an apprentice for Chelsea after he left school in the summer of 1957 and turned professional with the first team in 1960

when he was 17. He became captain and a pivotal player in a Chelsea club in the 60s which challenged for honours, notably winning the 1965 League Cup against Leicester City. He was a strong midfielder, with superb passing ability and hard in the tackle.

Venables had an argument with manager Tommy Docherty which led to an £80,000 transfer to Tottenham Hotspur in 1966. In 202 appearances for Chelsea he had scored 26 goals. Later he played for Queens's Park Rangers and Crystal Palace, where he moved into managing the team. In total he managed nine sides including Barcelona, where he acquired the name 'El Tel', and the England national squad.

Among his many other ventures, Venables is a television and newspaper pundit.

Terry Venables

PETER LESLIE OSGOOD

Osgood was born 1947 in Windsor, England, on the 20th of February and died on the 1st of March 2006.

Osgood came to Chelsea as a junior, making his debut at 17 years of age. The tall teenager's reputation for skillful goalscoring had gone before him, and he was soon a first team regular. In the League Cup on the 6th of October 1966, his leg was broken in a tackle by Emlyn Hughes and he missed Chelsea's first FA Cup final, when the Blues lost to Tottenham Hotspur 1—2.

'Ossie' returned from injury and resumed his graceful, skillful football. Although his talents were suited to the forward role, his ability to read the game and his impressive physical presence led manager Dave Sexton to play him in midfield for most of the 1968/69 season.

Despite Chelsea's up and downs, Osgood scored regularly, including a spectacular volley from outside the area against Arsenal, which was voted goal of the season in 1972/73.

Osgood made 380 appearances for Chelsea, scoring 150 goals and was one of just nine players to score in every round of the FA Cup.

There was a falling-out with manager Dave Sexton over the player's lifestyle, and he was placed on the transfer list. This lifestyle also earned the disapproval of Alf Ramsey, which prevented Osgood from putting his goalscoring talents to good use with the England squad. He was capped just four times by England in the early 1970s.

Known also as 'The King of Stamford Bridge' because of his exceptional talent and his personality, Osgood ran a pub, which failed, and was banned from Stamford Bridge by chairman Ken Bates for expressing criticism of the club. Years later, Abramovich reversed the ban, to Osgood's great relief. When Raquel Welch wore a T-shirt stating, *"I scored with Osgood"*, his status as a Chelsea legend was sealed and remains unrivalled to this day.

Ossie suffered a fatal heart attack on March the 1st 2006. His love for the club never wavered, and as a tribute to one of Chelsea's greats, his ashes were buried beneath the penalty spot at Stamford Bridge. A statue of the player now stands outside the west stand of the Stamford Bridge ground.

Peter Osgood
Bobby Tambling

BOBBY TAMBLING

Tambling was born on the 18th of September 1941. His talents were soon noticed by many top clubs and he joined Chelsea in 1957 at the age of 15. His debut came in 1959 when he scored against West Ham United. He soon became Chelsea's main striker and was their top goalscorer for five seasons during the 1960s.

Tambling always 'had his feet on the ground', a quiet man, who as a left-footer, was ignored by the England manager Alf Ramsey. He was also self- effacing, describing himself as an old banger in contrast to Jimmy Greaves, who was *".. a Rolls-Royce"*.

Ron Harris said of Tambling: *"Perhaps he wasn't the quickest fella on the pitch, but he would work all the game for the team, which was something we very much appreciated about him. Even when he was having a bad game, he would never go missing. He was the perfect player and the consummate professional"*.

In 1962, manager Tommy Docherty made him captain of the Chelsea side. His record for scoring the highest number of goals in one league match came during the game with Aston Villa on the 17th September 1966 when he scored 5 goals in Chelsea's 6-2 away win.

Tambling was named amongst the greatest XI players ever to play at Chelsea.

After leaving Chelsea, Tambling played for Crystal Palace and then moved to Ireland.

Tambling made 370 appearances scoring 202 goals in total.

RAY WILKINS

Wilkins was born on the 14th of September 1956. He was an apprentice with Chelsea, and with his obvious talents he made his first-team debut at the age of 17 against Norwich City on the 26th of October 1973 when he was a substitute. At the age of just 18, he became Chelsea's youngest-ever captain, taking over the position from long- standing captain Ron Harris and leading his team to promotion to the First Division after just one year in the second division.

He was the most outstanding player in the team, with his passing accuracy at long range pivotal in creating a stream of goal

opportunities for his teammates. His tendency to pass the ball sideways earned him the dubious nicknames of 'Squareball Wilkins', and 'The Crab'. He was also known for his spectacular long-range shots at goal.

Thanks to his *"dark good looks"*, Wilkins became a pinup in British teenager magazines of the period.

Wilkins left Chelsea in 1979 and moved to Manchester United. He has also played for A.C. Milan, Paris St. Germain and the England team. He soon became a permanent member of the national team, playing for them for the next decade.

Wilkins eventually moved into coaching and became assistant

Ray Wilkins

manager at Chelsea on two occasions between 1999 and 2000 and 2008 to 2010.

Wilkins can now be seen as a commentator on television.

DENNIS WISE

Wise was born on the 16th of December 1966 in Kensington, London. He joined the Chelsea team on the 3rd of July 1990 and spent the next eleven years of his career there. He was known for his combative play in midfield and became the player with the fourth most appearances for the club. He scored 76 goals in 445 matches and was top goalscorer during the 1991/92 season when he netted 14 goals. He was captain of the team when Chelsea won the FA Cup in 1997 and 2000 and the League Cup and UEFA Cup Winners Cup in 1998. In 1998 and 2000 he was voted Club Player of the Year.

Whilst at Chelsea, he was involved in disciplinary problems and controversy off the field which led to his being stripped of the Chelsea captaincy. Despite his personal faults, his leadership qualities were superb, and he made sure that the different natures of all the foreign players coming to Stamford Bridge in the 1990s gelled to form a coherent squad.

Wise later turned to managing and became manager of Swindon Town on the 22nd of May 2006, moving on to Leeds United the same year.

In 738 appearances, Wise scored 120 goals; 76 of those were for Chelsea in 445 appearances for the club.

GIANFRANCO ZOLA

Zola was born on the 5th of July 1966 in Oliena, Sardinia, Italy. He signed for Chelsea in November 1966, making his debut against Blackburn Rovers in a 1-1 draw. During the 1996/97 season, Zola was pivotal in Chelsea's revival which saw them win the FA Cup. Known for playing the game as though he truly enjoyed his time on the field, his ball skills were superb, with a 25 yard curling shot against Liverpool and a spectacular goal against Wimbledon when he back-heeled the ball, turned 180 degrees and scored, being just two of the most memorable

Dennis Wise

moments.

On the 13th of November 1991, Zola made his debut for Italy. He retired from the national team in 1998 having acquired 35 caps and scored 10 goals.

In the 2002/03 season, his final season with Chelsea, he was voted the club's player of the year, a distinction that he received twice. His final goal for the club on Easter Monday 2003, came from a ball lobbed in from outside the penalty area.

Fans voted Zola as the best ever Chelsea player, in 2003. In November 2004 he was awarded an OBE, and became one of the Chelsea F.C. Centenary Eleven, in 2005.

RUUD GULLIT

Gullit was born on the 1st of September 1962 in Amsterdam. His professional career started in 1978 when he signed for HFC Haarlem.

He made his international debut with the Netherlands national team on his 19th birthday in 1981, and became one of the key players in the Dutch side. Angered by being removed from his usual central position, Gullit walked out of the Dutch pre-tournament training camp for the 1994 FIFA World Cup and never returned to international football.

After seasons with PSV Eindhoven and Milan amongst others, he moved to Chelsea in July 1995, where he had only moderate success in the sweeper position. Once he was changed to midfield, his performances improved and despite finding the adjustment to the Chelsea style of playing difficult at first, he was named runner-up as Footballer of the Year. He was later quoted as saying that the matches at Chelsea were " … the only time I really had fun".

Gullit's talent was praised by none other than George Best. Best commented: *"Ruud Gullit is a great player by any standards. He has all the skills … That's what makes him an even better player than Maradona. Both have the key quality you will find in all the best players: balance".*

Comfortable in many positions on the pitch, Gullit was a first-class athlete, tall, and excellent in the air with powerful heading ability. His technique was second to none, and his clever use and understanding of

Gianfranco Zola
Ruud Gullit

83

the space around him, his passing skills and his cool-headed play with the ball, turned him into a legendary figure.

In the summer of 1996, Gullit became player-manager of Chelsea. In his first season, he led Chelsea to an FA Cup triumph, the club's first major trophy in 26 years. Following an argument with the club's board, Gullit left to become manager of Newcastle United.

Gullit scored 218 goals in 553 appearances. His awards include Netherlands Player of the Year; Dutch Footballer of the Year; Dutch Sportsman of the Year; UEFA Player of the Year; Silver Ball English League Player of the Year; Chelsea Player of the Year; Fifa 100.

JOHN TERRY

One of the greatest defenders of all time John George Terry was born on 7 December 1980 in Barking

John Terry

England. Terry plays centre back and is the captain of Chelsea in the Premier League although he is out of contract at the end of the 2013 — 2014 season. He also captained the England team from August 2006 to February 2010 and from March 2011 to February 2012.

Terry played his first Chelsea game on 28 October 1998 as a substitute. His first full start came later that season in an FA Cup third round match. He spent a period on loan to Nottingham Forest in 2000 to gain first team experience. Terry was UEFA Club Defender of the Year in 2005, 2008 and 2009.and PFA Players' Player of the Year in 2005.

Terry is without a doubt Chelsea's most successful captain, winning three Premier League titles, four FA Cups, two League Cups and a UEFA Champions League. He has made over 500 appearances for Chelsea and is also the club's all-time highest scoring defender. John Terry made his announcement of retirement from international football on 23 September 2012.

FRANK LAMPARD

Lampard was born on the 20th of June 1978 in Romford, Essex, and between 1989 and 1994 he attended Brentwood School, gaining eleven GCSEs. His football career began at West Ham United, where he joined the youth team in 1994. He joined Chelsea in 2001 after his father and also his uncle, Harry Redknapp, were fired by the West Ham, making his debut on August the 19th in a 1-1 draw against Newcastle United.

In September 2003, Lampard was named Barclays Player of the Month, and at the end of that season he had reached double goal figures in the league for the first time. In 2004/05 Lampard played in all 38 Premier League matches. It was the third consecutive season he had done so and his record stands at 164, a run which ended on the 28th of December 2005. The Barclays Player of the Season award went to him in 2005, too, as did the Footballer of the Year award.

In the 2005/06 season, Mourinho called him " ... the best player in the world", after he scored from a 25-yard free kick.

Another award, the UEFA Club Midfielder of the Year award was his

in 2007, which he followed up with being awarded the Premier League Player of the Month for the third time in October 2008. He has been Chelsea player of the Year three times, too.

His nomination as England Player of the Year — he has been capped 100 times — in 2004 and 2005 proves the extent of his talent.

Saturday May 11th, 2013, was a special day for Lampard. Not only did he score his 202nd goal for Chelsea, but also his 203rd. With that he became Chelsea's all-time best goalscorer, surpassing Bobby Tambling's record of 202. He is without doubt, Chelsea's greatest player.

Lampard is now reckoned to be one of the best English midfielders ever. Known for his phenomenal work-rate between the boxes, he is master of a range of passes and possesses a great ability to score goals.

Lampard has two children with Spanish model Elen Rivas; Luna and Isla.

TÉBILY DIDIER YVES DROGBA

Drogba was born on the 11th of March 1978 on the Ivory Coast, Africa, and at the age of five was sent to live in France with his uncle

85

Frank Lampard & Didier Drogba

in his career with accusations of diving and handling the ball. Yet his ability to target opposition players holding the ball, and involve teammates in the forward action, has been invaluable to the teams he has played for. He will probably be best remembered at Chelsea for his contribution in the Champions League final in Munich when he scored the winning goal against Bayern Munich in a penalty shootout.

Drogba is married to Diakité Lalla. They met in Paris and have 3 children. His younger brothers are also both footballers.

EDEN HAZARD

Eden Michael Hazard was born on the 7th of January 1991 in La Louvière, Belgium. Both his mother and father were footballers and later sports teachers. Hazard started playing for his home team at the age of four, and even then his talents were obvious and he was considered a gifted player. He was spotted by a talent scout, and with his parents permission, moved to Lille in Northern France.

He made his professional debut in November 2007 with the French club, becoming the youngest goalscorer in the club's history, and his international debut with the senior Belgian National side came in 2008.

Hazard is an attacking midfielder and winger and the 1.73m (5ft 8in) player has won the National Union of Professional Footballers Young Player of the Year Award twice, and he won the league and cup Double with Lille in the 2010/11 season.

Following years of interest from other clubs, Hazard joined Chelsea in June 2012 after an eight-year stint with in France, becoming the PFA Young Player of the Year in his second season. He also became top goalscorer for the 2013/14 season with 14 goals, and he scored the second best tally the following year with 15. In the 2106/17 season, he was also firing on all cylinders with 17 to his credit.

Hazard has always made his presence felt, often scoring goals at vital points in a match, as he did in his debut season for Chelsea against Manchester United in the FA Cup quarter finals.

During the 2016/17 season, Hazard was voted Premier League Player of the Month in October.

Amongst a vast array of other awards, Hazard was voted Chelsea Player of the Year in 2013/14, 2014/15 and 2016/17 besides receiving

Michel Goba, a professional footballer. Three years later he returned to Africa for a brief period, returning to France after his parents lost their jobs. He joined the semi- professional club Levallois, where his professionalism and prolific scoring ability made a great impression on his coach.

He first played for Côte d'Ivoire in 2002 and became captain of the Côte d'Ivoire national team in 2006. He is their top scorer.

His career at Chelsea began in 2004 where he moved after a record £24 million transfer fee. Scoring in his third appearance, he was in the team that won its first league title for 50 years. In 2006-07 he netted 33 goals, winning the Premier Golden Boot, and won the award again in 2010. His 100th goal came in March 2012.

Drogba is a powerful 6' 2" striker, who has attracted controversy

Eden Hazard

the UEFA Best Player in Europe Award for 2015, the FIFA Ballon d'Or: 8th place 2015, and scoring the Chelsea Goal of the Year for 2015 in the game against Tottenham Hotspur. As if that wasn't enough, he also boasts the award for FWA Footballer of the Year for 2014/15, PFA Players' Player of the Year for 2014/15 and PFA Young Player of the Year for 2013/14.

It's an impressive line up for a young player. Indeed, Hazard has been called the best player in the world on his day, his playing described as mesmerising, and astonishing, and he has been compared to none other than Lionel Messi. His finishing is first rate and he is blisteringly fast and it is all but impossible to part him from the ball.

DIEGO COSTA

Diego De Silva Costa was born on the 7th of October 1988 in Lagarto, Brazil. His first name was given to him in honour of Diego Maradona, the legendary Argentinian footballer.

At the age of 15, he went to work in São Paulo in his uncle's shop before joining the Barcelona Esportiva Capela team. Despite never having received football training, he became a professional with the club.

In February 2006 Costa signed for the Portuguese club Braga, but failed to make much of an impression.

There followed an odyssey through a variety of European clubs, where a reputation for poor conduct followed him, and he seemed to be on a downward slide when he started to become overweight.

The 2010/11 season found him with Atlético Madrid for the second time. During his time there, he was plagued by injuries and involved in on-field arguments.

Finally, rejecting an offer by Liverpool to join them, Costa showed his true worth in the 2013/14 season getting 27 league goals and eight goals during the Champions League campaign equalling a record held since 1959.

In July 2014, Chelsea announced that the player would be joining them for the new season. Even though he was troubled with his old hamstring injury, Costa was instrumental in helping Chelsea to

the league title win, netting 21 goals to become top goalscorer. He repeated the feat during the following difficult season with 12 goals to his credit. It was a season in which Costa, once again, was involved in physical arguments on the field, which brought him in a ban on more than one occasion — and the unfortunate accolade of the Premier League's dirtiest player.

Costa's physical strength, however — he's 1.88m (6ft 2in) tall — together with his ability to keep possession of the ball better than any Chelsea striker since Drogba, are two of his greatest assets, and his scoring skills have already brought him a welter of personal awards: the Copa del Rey: Top scorer 2012/13, La Liga Player of the Month in September 2013, La Liga Team of the Season for 2013/14, Trofeo EFE in 2013/14, UEFA Champions League Team of the Season in 2013/14, Premier League Player of the Month for August 2014 and November 2016, PFA Team of the Year in 2014/15.

Costa took Spanish citizenship in September 2013, and played his debut for the Spanish national side in March 2014.

Diego Costa

87

THE MANAGERS

A brief list of Chelsea managers

DAVID CALDERHEAD

Calderhead was born on the 19th of June 1864 in Hurlford, Scotland, and died on the 9th of January 1938 in London.

Calderhead became Chelsea's secretary—manager in 1907 staying with the club for 26 years, which makes him the club's longest-serving manager. Under his command, the team were relegated twice, and promoted twice.

The manager, who earned the nickname, *"The Sphinx of Stamford Bridge"*, due to his reluctance to speak to the media, was not greatly involved in the day-to-day training of the team. But he was responsible for bringing in many star players such as Hughie Gallacher, and holds the record for the number of games for a manager at Chelsea; 966.

Calderhead's death at the age of 73 came five years after he left Chelsea.

EDWARD JOSEPH "TED" DRAKE

Drake was born on the 16th of August 1912 and died on the 30th of May 1995.

Drake made his debut as a player for Southampton, and made a name for himself in the 1930s when he played for Arsenal. He took over the managership of Chelsea in 1952 when they were in the First Division.

Drake made radical changes to the way the team was run and improved the club's image. Chelsea had been seen as a rather amateurish team supported by trendy Londoners, rather than a serious football club. Under his stewardship, the 'Pensioners' nickname disappeared and the Lion Rampant Regardant and the nickname, 'The Blues', came in. It took just 3 years for Drake to bring Chelsea their first ever league championship trophy, which came in the 1954/55 season. This made him the first person to lift the league title as both a player and a manager. Despite the emergence of talented young players such as Jimmy Greaves and Bobby Tambling, Drake never again achieved the success of his former years and was sacked early in the 1961/62 season.

↑ **David Calderhead**
Ted Drake

He then became reserve team manager at Fulham. He was 82 years old when he died.

THOMAS HENDERSON "TOMMY" DOCHERTY

Docherty was born on the 24th of April 1928 in Gorbals, Glasgow, Scotland.

As a player his most notable appearances were for Preston North End, but he also played 25 times for the Scottish national team. In 1961, he became Chelsea's manager.

Docherty introduced blue shorts to the team's colours, and Chelsea became known as 'Docherty's Diamonds'. He led them back into the First Division after his first full season at the club and put together a team that included stars such as Peter Osgood, Charlie Cook, Peter Bonetti, and Ron Harris, playing fast-flowing football.

Charlie Cooke said of Docherty: *"Tommy Docherty was full of bounce, full of fun, always looking for a joke, real fun to be around"*.

He was a controversial, combative figure, however, and following an allegation of racial abuse during a tour of Bermuda, he resigned in October 1967.

He then managed a series of teams, including Queens Park Rangers, Aston Villa, Manchester United and Wolverhampton Wanderers.

Docherty's final season of management came in 1987/88.

JOSÉ MÁRIO DOS SANTOS MOURINHO FÉLIX

José Mourinho was born on the 26th of January 1963 in Setúbal, Portugal. His father, Félix Mourinho, was goalkeeper for the Portuguese national team. When he was a teenager, José would travel to see his father play, and once his father became a coach, the youngster received his first coaching lessons by observing his father's training methods. He also made himself useful by scouting opposing teams. And there was a lesson on the harsh realities of football that he would come up against himself, later in life: "I was nine or 10 years old", said Mourinho years later, "and my father was sacked on Christmas Day. He was a manager; the results had not been good, he lost a game on December the 22nd or 23rd. On Christmas Day, the telephone rang and he was sacked in the middle of our lunch."

89

After leaving school, the young 5ft 9in (1.74m) José wanted to be a professional footballer, too, and joined the Beleneses youth team. At senior level he played for the team where his father was a coach, Rio Ave, but realised at the age of 23 that he did not possess enough power or speed to be truly effective on the field. Encouraged by his mother, Maria Júlia, Mourinho enrolled in business school but dropped out after just one day, going instead to study sports science at the Instituto Superior de Educacao Físcia (ISEF) where he earned his degree in exercise science, delivering a thesis on the methodology of soccer. He then taught physical education for five years in a variety of schools and — chalking up consistently good results — earned his diploma. It was when he took courses in football coaching conducted by the English and Scottish Football Associations that his methods of combining motivational and psychological techniques with coaching theory took shape.

In 1989, Mourinho married the woman that he had met when they were both teenagers in Setúbal. Her name was Matilde 'Tami' Faria, who was born in Angola. "The most important thing is my family and being a good father", said Mourinho later, stating that his family is the centre of his life. He and Matilde have two children; Matilde and José Mário.

In 1992, Mourinho accepted a job as translator to Sir Bobby Robson, the new manager of Lisbon club, Sporting CP.

Mourinho and Robson discussed coaching and tactics as part of his job as interpreter, and when Robson moved to FC Porto, Mourinho went with him and served in the same role at the new club.

In 1996 Robson and Mourinho went to FC Barcelona, where Mourinho began assisting players in analysing opposing teams. When Robson left the club, Mourinho stayed on and became assistant to the new manager, Louis van Gaal. Mourinho's talent was evident, and the new manager allowed him to develop his own style of coaching, leaving the FC Barcelona B team entirely in his care. Van Gaal also generously allowed Mourinho to take charge of the first-team in some of the competitions.

Speaking about this period of his life at Barcelona, Mourinho said: "I was more influenced by Barca's philosophy than by any other coach. They were four years of my life absolutely fundamental." (sic)

In September 2000, Mourinho was given his first permanent management role when he took over at Benfica. But after just nine league games as manager, Mourinho resigned on the 5th of December 2000 when the club refused to extend his contract.

In April 2001, Mourinho took over at Uniã de Leiria, helping them to finish in 5th position, the club's highest league placing ever. His achievement caught the attention of Portugal's best clubs, and by January 2002 he had moved to Futebol Clube do Porto, known as FC Porto.

It was at Porto that Mourinho's distinctive coaching style became evident when his defenders and midfielders used their physical attacking talents to pressurise their opponents, who then either lost the ball or were forced into long, unreliable passes. The results were dramatic and proof of Mourinho's unique abilities. In their first season, 2002/03, led by Mourinho's flamboyant personality and superb coaching skills, Porto won the triple of the domestic League, (Primeira Liga) the Portuguese Cup and UEFA Cup titles.

These were followed up with further success in 2004; the Toyota Cup and the UEFA Champions League title. Porto had downed Mourinho's future rivals Manchester United along the way. Speaking about that victory and manager Alex Ferguson, Mourinho made it clear in a statement that expressed his own justified pride in his achievements, why many other managers are irked by what is seen as his arrogance. Mourinho said, "I understand why he is a bit emotional. He has some top players in the world and they should be doing a lot better ... you would be sad if your team gets as clearly dominated by opponents who have been built on ten percent of the budget."

The Portuguese had become a true leader and guide to his players. His knowledge of the game and attacking football is unparalleled, and he will defend his players to the hilt, rightly or wrongly. This was proven when he was at Inter and said of one former Chelsea player, "I am no longer Chelsea coach, and I do not have to defend them any more, so I think it is correct if I say Drogba is a diver."

In June 2004 Mourinho, began his legendary career at Chelsea. At a press conference that year he was quoted as saying, " ... please don't call me arrogant, but I'm European champion and I think I'm a special one". This led to him being nicknamed "The Special One". The nickname spawned a cartoon in his home country. His £4.2 million salary meant that he was one of the highest-paid managers in football and one year later this had been raised to 5.2 million.

He is certainly a strong-minded and charismatic character, and his relationship with the press has been tempestuous. Acknowledging his difficult nature, he said of himself, "It's hard to keep up with my ego, but the players just have to live with it."

He is known for his sophisticated fashion sense, and his stylish appearance has meant that he has found fame of a different kind, as he has often been seen on the front pages of newspapers and is a topic in the gossip columns. He is also resident in Madame Tussaud's in London.

Bankrolled by Roman Abramovich, Mourinho set about building a Chelsea side that could win trophies. He brought in players from all over the world such as Didier Drogba, Tiago, Ricardo Carvalho and Paulo Ferreira. His talent in moulding these disparate talents into a winning team soon became evident. Two games into his managership he had introduced his favoured team constellation; 4-3-3. He likes to place 3 men up front, 2 in wide positions and 3 in the central areas with two defensive midfielders as the core of the team and one attacker free to roam.

By December of 2005, Chelsea were top of the Premier League table. The first trophy arrived when Chelsea beat Liverpool 3—2 in the League Cup. Records were not long in coming either; most points ever in the Premier League, 95, fewest goals conceded, 15. Mourinho was voted Coach of the Year in the BBC Sports Personality of the Year Awards for 2005. And not only did Mourinho steer Chelsea to the Premiership in 2004/05 and 2005/06, he was also voted Premiership Manager of the Year in both seasons. On top of that, he was named the world's best football manager by the International Federation of Football History and Statistics (IFFHS) in the 2004-05 and 2005-06 seasons.

By the end of the season in 2006, Chelsea had beaten rivals Manchester United 3—0 and won their 2nd consecutive Premiership. For Mourinho, it was the 4th successive domestic title.

The 2006-07 season was marred by a deterioration in the relationship between Mourinho and Abramovich although Chelsea still managed to win the League Cup and then the FA Cup final against Manchester United, 1—0. Despite their professional rivalry, Mourinho confessed to being a fan of Sir Alex Ferguson's, and away from the pitch the two are friends. The methods of the two men also show similarities which are part of their success stories. "The team", said Mourinho, "is completely closed. Anything you say outside, there is no chance it will go inside. So the team is really strong and compact. We know what we want and how to achieve it on the pitch."

The disagreements between the Chelsea manager and the owner continued into the new season 2007—08. After a less successful start, Mourinho suddenly left the club on the 20th of September 2007. He had been Chelsea's most successful manager since the club's foundation in 1905, and the team had won six trophies in three years without losing a single league game at home. Without doubt, he had brought together a side that he had formed into the best team in the country.

Mourinho joined Internazionale in June 2008. His sometimes brusque manner also caused controversy in Italy, as it did when he accused Italian sports journalists of "intellectual prostitution", and verbally insulted rival clubs.

During his tenure at Inter Milan, which many consider to be a 'golden era', for the club, Mourinho brought the club to new heights. Inter became the first Italian club to win the treble, after beating Bayern Munich 2-0 in the Champions League final; the Serie A, Coppa Italia and the UEFA Champions League were theirs.

Another record came Mourinho's way on the 6th of April 2010, when he became the first manager in history to take three different teams to the semi-finals of the UEFA Champions League. Internazionale had overcome CSKA Moscow 0—1 in Russia in the second leg of their quarter-final tie, which ended 2—0 on aggregate.

At the time, Mourinho described Inter Milan's Champions League semi-final victory over Barcelona, 3-2 on aggregate, on the 29th April 2010 as " ... the greatest moment of my career". There was also room for humour. "It is clear", he said, "that I will end my career without having coached Barca."

The win over Bayern Munich had made him only the third manager to win the Champions League with two different clubs.

Mourinho's talents were recognised when he won the Panchina d'Oro, Coach of the Year award, in Italy for 2009/10.

Mourinho was apparently considering the managership at Manchester United once Sir Alex Ferguson retired. On the 28th of May 2010, however, he joined Real Madrid, the team which brought him his greatest winning margin,

8—0, against Levante. "If you don't coach Real Madrid then you will always have a gap in your career", was his comment on the move.

He guided the team to a Copa del Rey victory in his first season there and helped the team to win the Spanish La Liga title for the second time in four years.

Under his leadership, they also set records for the most points achieved by any team in the top European leagues, 100, most games won in a La Liga season, 32, finishing the season with the highest goal difference, 89, and improving on the previous record of most goals scored, 121. By 2013, Mourinho had won every Spanish domestic title within the space of two years and claimed an astonishing record of winning every domestic title in four European leagues;

Mourinho continued to have fraught relationships with some of his players. The dispute with Sergio Ramos and club captain Iker Castillas, divided the "Mourinhistas" from the "Madridistas", who were the more traditional Real Madrid fans. Cristiano Ronaldo also had problems with his manager, with Mourinho accusing Ronaldo of being too precious to take criticism.

There were also other controversial incidents, such as poking assistant Barca coach Tito Vilanova in the eye during a brawl, whilst the complaints about biased referees and the clashes with journalists and Real officials went on throughout Mourinho's tenure. At the end of the 2012/13 season, he described it as, " … the worst of my career". It was announced that the manager would leave the club.

On June the 13th came the announcement that Mourinho was returning to the Chelsea fold. He said, "In my career I've had two great passions — Inter and Chelsea — and Chelsea is more than important for me."

Outside of football, Mourinho's charity work includes a youth project, where he uses football to bring together Palestinian and Israeli children. His quick mind is evident elsewhere, too, for he speaks six languages; English, French, Italian, Catalan, Spanish and Portuguese.

Pepe Guardiola, manager of Bayern Munich, said of Mourinho that he was, " … probably the best coach in the world", and many critics, players and coaches would agree. Chelsea's long-serving midfielder Frank Lampard considers Mourinho to be the best manager he has ever worked for. And for all his criticism of opposing managers, coaches and teams, Mourinho has not

spared the praise when he felt it was due. He once said of Arsenal: " (They) have won that advantage, nobody gave it to them. By playing fantastic football and by winning matches and by winning trophies, they won that respect that the opponent has for them."

Mourinho has always been able to motivate and infuse his teams with the will to win, to transfer his own self-confidence to the players, an ability that has made him one of the great names in football, a legend in his own lifetime.

In his own words: "The moral of the story is not to listen to those who tell you not to play the violin but stick to the tambourine."

Mourinho's awards:

- Onze d'Or Coach of the Year: 2005, 2010
- FIFA Ballon d'Or World Coach of the Year: 2010 (Mourinho auctioned this trophy and donated the proceeds to The Sir Bobby Foundation and Breakthrough Breast Cancer, in memory of his early mentor, Sir Bobby Robson, who died aged 76 in 2009.)
- IFFHS World's Best Club Coach: 2004, 2005, 2010, 2012
- Primeira Liga Manager of the Year: 2002/03, 2003/04
- Premier League Manager of the Year: 2004/05, 2005/06
- Premier League Manager of the Month: November 2004, January 2005, March 2007
- Serie A Manager of the Year: 2008/9, 2009/10
- Albo Panchina d'Oro: 2009/10
- Miguel Muñoz Trophy: 2010/11, 2011/12
- UEFA Manager of the Year: 2002/03, 2003/04
- UEFA Team of the Year: 2003, 2004, 2005, 2010
- World Soccer Magazine World Manager of the Year: 2004, 2005, 2010
- LPFP Awards Best Portuguese Manager in Foreign Countries: 2008/09, 2009/10
- BBC Sports Personality of the Year Coach Award: 2005
- La Gazzetta dello Sport Man of the Year: 2010
- International Sports Press Association Best Manager in the World: 2010
- Prémio Prestígio Fernando Soromenho: 2012
- Officer of the Order of Infante Dom Henrique;
- Honoris causa — an honorary degree awarded by the Technical University of Lisbon for his achievements in football;
- Football Extravaganza's League of Legends;

GUUS HIDDINK

Hiddink was born on the 8th of November 1946 in Varsseveld in the Netherlands.

Following a long career as a player in midfield, Hiddink then turned to coaching in 1982, and his talents met with great success both at home and abroad, being acknowledged by the Dutch when they gave him a turn at the helm of the Dutch national team.

It was during his time at PSV Eindhoven between 2002 and 2006 that he became the most successful manager in Dutch football history.

Hiddink was managing the Russian national squad when he accepted the appointment as Chelsea FC's interim coach for the remainder of the 2008/09 season. He led the team in a thrilling return to form in which they only lost one match under his leadership.

When José Mourinho was given his marching orders in 2015, the club turned to Hiddink once again; and once again they were rewarded; this time with a 12-match unbeaten run. This was a record for the new manager of a team. As interim manager, Hiddink was replaced by Antonio Conte for the 2016/17 season.

A host of managerial awards given to Hiddink include:

- **AFC Coach of the Year: 2002.**
- **World Soccer World Manager of the Year: 2002.**
- **Dutch Sports Coach of the Year (all sports): 2002, 2005.**
- **Rinus Michels Award: 2005, 2006.**
- **Coach of the Year in Russia: 2008.**
- **Honorary doctorate from the University of Seoul 2005.**
- **An honorary citizen of Seoul.**
- **An honorary citizen of Eindhoven.**
- **Hiddink was put on a stamp by the Australian Post Office following the 2006 FIFA World Cup.**
- **Lifetime achievement award by the Royal Dutch Football Association in 2007.**
- **He won the FA Cup in 2008/09 with Chelsea**

Guus Hiddink

ANTONIO CONTE

Conte was born on the 31st of July 1969 in Lecce in Italy. Conte began his playing career as a central midfielder going on to celebrate enormous success with Juventus, a team he led to the field as captain. In 1994, he was called to the national team at the age of 24. Considered an excellent and powerful player, his leadership skills, stamina and ability to read the game were his greatest assets.

Hanging up his playing boots in 2006, he became manager to Siena, Arezzo and Bari, and although success did not come instantly, in the 2008/09 season he led Bari to the Serie B title.

He returned to Juventus as their manager and in laying down the law to them in no uncertain terms, guided them to three Serie A titles. He then took over the Italian national team.

On April the 4th, 2016, Conte was appointed as manager of Chelsea with a three-year contract and he started out in September 2016 as he meant to continue: with a 2-1 home win against West Ham. His obvious flair and instinct for success were soon rewarded with a six-game unbeaten run and the Premier League Manager of the Month award in October 2016.

Conte favours the 3-5-2 formation, and it has stood him in good stead, because by the end of December, he had set a club record of thirteen consecutive victories.

In the first months of his tenure, the comparisons to other managerial greats came in thick and fast; comparisons to Alex Ferguson and José Mourinho, for example. One Italian player said of him that he had *"… fire running through his veins and he moved like a viper"*.

Which all bodes extremely well for Chelsea's future.

Conte's individual awards so far include:

- **The Panchina d'Argento for 2008/09.**
- **The Panchina d'Oro in 2011/12, 2012/13 and 2013/14.**
- **The Serie A Coach of the Year in: 2011/12, 2012/13 and 2013/14.**
- **The Trofeo Tommaso Maestrelli for the Best Italian Manager in 2011/12.**
- **The Globe Soccer Award for the Best Coach of the Year in 2013.**
- **The Premier League Manager of the Month for October 2016, November 2016 and December 2016.**
- **London Football Awards for Manager of the Year, 2017.**
- **Premier League Manager of the Year, 201/17.**
- **LMA Manager of the Year, 2016/17.**